CONCEPTS IN WESTERN THOUGHT SERIES

The Idea of Justice

CONCEPTS IN WESTERN THOUGHT SERIES

GENERAL EDITOR: MORTIMER J. ADLER

INSTITUTE FOR PHILOSOPHICAL RESEARCH

The
Idea
of
Justice

by

Otto A. Bird

FREDERICK A. PRAEGER, *Publishers*
New York • Washington • London

FREDERICK A. PRAEGER, PUBLISHERS
111 Fourth Avenue, New York, N.Y. 10003, U.S.A.
77–79 Charlotte Street, London W.1, England

Published in the United States of America in 1967
by Frederick A. Praeger, Inc., Publishers

© 1967 by Institute for Philosophical Research

Library of Congress Catalog Card Number: 67–20472

Printed in the United States of America

Coniugi meae bene dilectae
Animae dimidio meae

*Persons Engaged in the Work of
the Institute for Philosophical Research
1961–1967*

RESEARCH STAFF
SENIOR FELLOWS

Mortimer J. Adler

———————

Otto A. Bird
William J. Gorman

Robert G. Hazo
V. J. McGill
A. L. H. Rubin
Charles Van Doren

RESEARCH ASSOCIATES

Betty Beck Bennett
Ann Quinn Burns
Paul Cornelius
Katherine Farnsworth
Ross Firestone

Edgar V. Meyer
Harvey Meyers
Charles T. Sullivan
Gerald Temaner
Jeffrey Weiss

ADMINISTRATIVE AND CLERICAL STAFF

Marlys A. Buswell
Helen M. Kresich
Theresa A. Panek
Denise Ryan

Carter Nelson Sullivan
Frances S. Ward
Celia Wittenber

BOARD OF DIRECTORS
INSTITUTE FOR PHILOSOPHICAL RESEARCH

Mortimer J. Adler
Mortimer Fleishhacker, Jr.,
    Chairman
Robert P. Gwinn
Prentis C. Hale
Daggett Harvey

Louis Kelso
Harold F. Linder
Arthur L. H. Rubin
Hermon D. Smith
Leonard Spacek

Acknowledgments

The clarification of the idea of justice that is here offered to the public is the work of the Institute for Philosophical Research. As author, I have been but *primus inter pares* and first only as the one responsible for directing the research and presenting the results that have been achieved. The initial conception of the project as well as the method for carrying it out were the result of a common effort. So, too, the actual analysis of the extensive literature devoted to the subject of justice would not have been possible without the collaborative work of many. Even the final shape here given to the results would not have been achieved without the unfailing and expert criticism of the members of the staff and especially of Mortimer J. Adler and William J. Gorman.

I would also like to express gratitude to my philosophical colleagues, especially at the University of Notre Dame, for the many illuminating discussions I had with them about theories of justice.

OTTO A. BIRD

South Bend, Indiana
December, 1966

Foreword

The Idea of Justice is one of a series of studies of basic ideas undertaken by the Institute for Philosophical Research. The Institute was established in 1952 with the avowed purpose of taking stock of Western thought on subjects that have been of continuing philosophical interest from the advent of philosophy in ancient Greece to the present day. In pursuing this task, it hopes to clarify the recorded discussion of such basic ideas as freedom, justice, happiness, love, progress, equality, and law. It aims to transform what, in every case, at first appears to be a chaos of differing opinions into an orderly set of clearly defined points of agreement and disagreement that give rise to real issues and make possible the kind of rational debate that constitutes genuine controversy.

What we are given to start with in each case is a diversity of opinions, the pattern of which is seldom clear. To put order into that diversity and to render it intelligible require a creative effort to construct the controversies that are implicit in it. Only by an explicit formulation of the pattern of agreements and disagreements, together with the reasons for the latter, can we delineate the issues and indicate how they have been or might be disputed. Too often reasons have not been given for positions that have been persistently advanced. In consequence, important issues have not been disputed in a way that carries the controversy forward and brings it nearer to a resolution.

The Institute has proceeded on the assumption that the issues in the field of any basic philosophical idea concern matters about which objective truth is ascertainable. The future resolution of these issues depends upon more sustained and more rational efforts to deal with them than the history of Western thought has so far exhibited; and the initiation of such efforts depends in turn upon a clear and precise understanding of the issues. Providing this has been the sole aim of the Institute's work from the beginning.

To accomplish its aim, the Institute has developed certain procedures and a distinctive method of work. Its approach to the study of the recorded discussion of basic philosophical ideas is essentially dialectical. The materials being studied—the major documents in the literature of any philosophical subject—are historical in the sense that each has a date and place in the history of thought about that subject; but the Institute's study of these materials is *non-historical* in aim. It deliberately abstracts from their historical context and pattern. It views them as if they were all contemporary—as if the documents represented the voices of participants confronting one another in actual discussion. The Institute's approach is also *non-philosophical* in the sense that it does not undertake to develop or defend a theory of the idea under consideration. The only truth with which the Institute is directly concerned is truth concerning the body of thought about a particular subject, not truth about the subject thought about. The Institute, therefore, refrains from taking part in the discussion that it attempts to clarify. It makes a sustained effort to be impartial in its treatment of all points of view and to deal with them in an objective and neutral manner. It strives to function as a detached bystander or impartial observer, not as a critic or judge assessing the merits of conflicting claims and awarding a verdict.

It should be clear why an intellectual enterprise thus designed and directed is facilitated by a collaborative effort under institutional auspices; it would be almost impossible for a single person working alone to accomplish effectively. On any basic idea, the volume of literature to be examined and interpreted is tremendous, even if only the most significant and representative documents are selected for study. In the process of interpretation and in the attempt to treat all points of view with impartiality, the desired neutrality is more likely to be achieved by many individuals working together than by the most determined effort of a single individual. Collaboration and consultation tend to offset the idiosyncrasies of individual temperaments and intellectual biases. The advantage of teamwork is not only the pooling of diverse abilities, but also the correction of blind spots and the checking of prejudices.

The first product of the collaborative effort of the Institute's staff was a two-volume study, *The Idea of Freedom*, Volume I of which was published in 1958, and Volume II in 1961. That study exemplified the Institute's dialectical method in the treatment of a basic idea, and its results provided a good measure of what can be achieved by the application of that method. The present study, *The Idea of Justice*, represents an adaptation of the same method to the treatment of another basic idea. Like *The Idea of Freedom*, it is a product of the collaborative efforts of the Institute's staff. While the task of writing this book was undertaken by one member of the staff, Dr. Otto Bird, a team formed from other members of the staff helped in the examination and interpretation of the literature under consideration; the formulations proposed by Dr. Bird were checked and criticized by his colleagues; and the manuscript was revised in accordance with suggestions made by them. The names of the collaborators specifically engaged in the production of the present volume, together with the names of other members of the Institute's staff and of its Board of Directors, will be found facing the acknowledgments page.

The construction of the controversy concerning justice set forth in this book approximates the dialectical ideal of what controversy should be like. The reader who carefully examines the table of contents of Dr. Bird's book will see at once that all the formal requisites of controversy are satisfied—an identifiable subject of discussion, a set of questions that elicit answers from the major authors who discuss the subject, several theories (in this case three) of justice that take positions on each of the issues raised by those questions and, in terms of the complex pattern of agreements and disagreements that emerges from the positions they take, constitute a three-sided controversy about justice.

The work that the Institute has done on the ideas of freedom, progress, happiness, and love has clarified the discussion and ordered the diversity of views on each of those ideas, but it has not eventuated in the formulation of a controversy that is nearly as well-structured as is the one here presented in the case of justice. This striking difference stems, in our judgment, not from the character of the work done by Dr. Bird, but rather from the character of the idea on which he worked. In our study of a half dozen or more great ideas, we have found that the universe of discourse centering on each idea is a world of its own, distinguished by features that are characteristic of it and no other idea. The idea of justice is distinguished by the fact that the discussion of it exhibits a clearer pattern of agreements and disagreements and a more orderly set of issues about a commonly agreed upon subject than any other idea on which we have so far worked.

Unfortunately, the literature concerned with the idea of justice does not fully live up to the ideal of rational controversy. While the three main theories that it presents enabled Dr. Bird to formulate genuine issues in a well-structured controversy about them, the literature did not afford him the materials out of which to construct a well-argued debate of these issues. For the most part, the exponents of each of the three main theories do not go much further than take positions on the questions at issue, with some show of argument for the positions that they take; but the exponents of one theory seldom, if ever, argue explicitly against the positions taken by the adherents of the other two; nor do they argue in defense of their own positions against contrary views. If even one exponent of each of the three main theories had understood the controversial situation as it is outlined in this book, and with that in mind had engaged explicitly in dispute with his acknowledged adversaries, we might have here an extraordinary —and quite exceptional—realization of the ideal of rational debate concerning a great idea. We are at least entitled to hope that Dr. Bird's book may lead to this result in future discussions of justice. In any case, it cannot help improving the discussion of the subject; and just as *The Idea of Progress* illuminates issues that are pivotal in the philosophy of history, so *The Idea of Justice* throws light on questions that are central in the philosophy of law.

The Institute for Philosophical Research was established on grants from the Ford Foundation and the Old Dominion Foundation. When the Ford Foundation grant expired in 1956, the Old Dominion Foundation continued to support the Institute's work and was subsequently joined by other benefactors. I wish to express the Institute's gratitude to the sources of financial support that made it possible for it to complete its work on the idea of freedom after the expiration of the Ford grant, and beyond that to produce not only the present work on the idea of justice, but also studies of the idea of progress, the idea of love, and the idea of happiness. These four studies are now being published simultaneously. Other studies, one on the idea of equality and one on language and thought, are currently being undertaken and should be ready for publication in the near future.

In the period since 1962, the following foundations have made substantial contributions to the Institute: the Old Dominion Foundation, the Houghton Foundation, the General Service Foundation, the Liberal Arts Foundation, the Olive Bridge Foundation, and the Paul Jones Foundation. These acknowledgments would not be complete without an expression of special gratitude for the friendship and support of three men in particular—Paul Mellon and Ernest Brooks, Jr., of the Old Dominion Foundation, and Arthur Houghton, Jr., of the Houghton Foundation.

MORTIMER J. ADLER

Chicago
May, 1967

Contents

I

The Subject
and
Its Issues

I

The Subject of the Controversy

JUSTICE is a large subject with many topics and subtopics that have a vast range of significance. The greatness of its scope appears from the mere size and diversity of the treatises that have been devoted to it. Some authors, like Plato in *The Republic*, make it coterminous with all of virtue and the good life. When it is restricted in scope and treated as a special virtue, as it is by Aquinas, the subject may still cover a great many topics. The treatise devoted to justice in the *Summa Theologica* considers, among other topics, the nature of right; restitution and when it is mandatory; respect of persons; injury done to another, whether by deed or by word; cheating; usury; the virtue of religion and its opposites; piety to parents and to one's country; the special virtues of obedience, gratitude, vengeance, truth, friendliness, liberality, equity; and whether or not all of the Ten Commandments are precepts of justice. The theological character of his work leads Aquinas to consider many questions that other writers omit entirely from their analyses of justice. One of the reasons his work is so large, however, is common to all the larger books devoted to the subject, and

3

that is the extensive examination of what is the just thing to do in the circumstances of actual life. Kant, for instance, in *The Science of Right,* discusses such concrete questions as the rights and duties of property, of marriage, of contracts, and of war and peace—each of which is a large subject in itself.

The literature on the subject is immense. Justice has long been a subject of discussion among the learned, especially in law, philosophy, and theology. But the discussion is not limited to the learned alone. In fact, it is difficult to imagine any man who does not at one time or another have occasion to appeal to justice, and to question and discuss whether or not a given course of action or a law is just. The common man may not indulge in speculation about the meaning of justice, but he does not hesitate to use the concept or term.

Given the vastness of the subject and the extensiveness of its consideration, it is not surprising that the word "justice" and its cognates have come to be used in many different ways and to be applied to a large range of objects. Grammatically, justice-words take many forms: adjective, adverb, noun, verb, or auxiliary in compounds with other words.

We use the adjective "just" to refer to the character of the man in the street as well as to that of men in special office—the judge, the legislator, the ruler. Besides applying it to the man himself or to his character, we also use it to qualify the actions he performs, the law he is governed by, the political society of which he is a member, the economy in which he earns his living, and the war in which he fights. Besides man's actions, we also use it for his words. We speak of the *"mot juste,"* and of a "just translation." We use it for thinking and its results in sentences, decisions, conclusions, inferences; and even for emotions and motives, as when we say of a man that "his fears and hopes proved just," or that he had "just cause to weep."

The uses of "justice" as a noun are almost as many and diverse. We apply it to the administration of the law, when we speak of "courts of justice," as well as to its administrators, "Supreme Court justice," or "justice of the peace." It also signifies the quality of character and disposition of one who is just. It appears in combination with other words: We "do justice" to a great variety of things: to other men, to a dinner, to a bottle of wine, to a topic or subject, to another's writing or thinking, to oneself, to one's emotions, etc.

The adverbial use of "just" is equally diverse and seemingly different from all the foregoing. We use it of time or event when we arrive at "just the wrong moment," or when one was "just at the point of death"; of position in hitting a person "just where it hurts most"; of manner and degree in "just the same," "just right," "it just fits."

We also have a verbal cognate in the word "justify," which has some of the uses of "just," but not all. A war can be described as "just," and we can also be asked to "justify it." A grocer may deal out "just weights and measures of his produce," and yet he is not asked to "justify his measure," although he could conceivably be asked to "adjust" his scales. Of the things that we "do justice to," some we can "justify," but not others. We can ask a person to "justify his interpretation" of a law or of an author, but it makes no sense to ask one to "justify his dinner or a bottle of wine."

The noun "justice" is itself qualified with different adjectives, and the result is often used to name different kinds of justice. These distinctions also serve to show the range of its applications, the many objects with which it is thought to deal. Man and his actions can be considered in relation to other men as individuals, or to the family, or to society at large and its laws, and then justice is characterized as commutative, domestic, social, or legal. We may look at society in its relations with its members, its lawbreakers, its economy, and with other states, and speak accordingly of distributive justice, of criminal or corrective justice, of economic justice, and of international justice.

Man and his various associations by no means exhaust the objects to which justice is applied. Some consider the existence of a toothache or of any pain as evidence of the injustice of nature or of God. The poet talks of "the most just earth" (*justissima tellus*), and he is allowed the exercise of "poetic justice" in allotting to his characters what each of them deserves, to assure that each "gets what's coming to him."

With so many diverse and divergent uses it is no cause for wonder that justice has become a subject of extensive controversy. The bibliography of the subject is bewildering in size and complexity. The actual literature dealing with justice is still more confusing. Almost three centuries ago, Leibniz lamented that "the notions of right and justice are still far from clear despite the fact that the clearest writers have written about them."[1] Since his day, many more books have been written about justice, and the list is still growing. Yet in all the

---

[1] Qu. in Del Vecchio, *Justice: An Historical and Philosophical Essay*, p. 2, Note 1.

discussion about justice, surprisingly little effort has been made to clarify and simplify the immense literature by attempting to locate and identify the various points at which major agreements and disagreements occur. Textbooks of jurisprudence usually have something to say about the various theories of justice, but for a systematic account of the whole literature only two works call for special mention. One, the work of Julius Stone, *Human Law and Human Justice* (1965), is the most recent survey of the field as a whole. The other is the small book by the late Giorgio Del Vecchio, *Justice: An Historical and Philosophical Essay*, which went through six editions from 1924, when the first appeared, until the last in 1959. Both men know well and closely the literature dealing with justice, and Del Vecchio, on his death, left one of the greatest libraries on jurisprudence ever collected.

Both men set out to analyze and compare the various theories of justice, and it might appear at first that our task is the same as theirs. Yet inspection will show that neither Del Vecchio nor Stone is attempting to simplify and clarify the controversy over justice in the way aimed at in this book. Neither is aiming at a dialectical clarification of the idea of justice. Their interests are primarily historical and philosophical rather than dialectical. In analyzing the literature on justice, they want, on the one hand, to provide a scrupulously faithful interpretation of the various authors they study, often given in the author's own special terminology. On the other hand, both writers are concerned to develop and advance their own particular theory of justice. They use what others have written about justice to advance their own account of it. They make some effort to compare the various theories with one another, to locate the points at which they meet and at which they part, but they do so in order to illuminate some feature, as they see it, of justice itself, and not of the controversy about justice. Their main aim is to state their own theory of justice, not to provide a simple and clear map of the controversy as a whole, which locates the basic positions that men have taken about the nature of justice.

To provide such a map is the task of this book. This map, once obtained, will provide what I have called a dialectical clarification of its subject. I call it this in order to distinguish it from a philosophical analysis of justice, on the one side, and from an historical analysis of the various theories, on the other. The object of this book is not to present another theory of justice but rather to analyze the controversy that arises among the various theories in the literature about it. Also, while it is true that the various theories occurring in the literature provide the material, the purpose in analyzing them is to show what the controversy is about, what its main issues are, and where the theories agree and disagree, and not to interpret the theories for their own sake. For the kind of clarification that is aimed at here, any theory of justice contains subtleties and complexities, special insights often expressed in a special terminology which, however valuable they may be in themselves, are largely irrelevant to the task of plotting the general shape of the whole controversy. In fact, their very complexity may readily impede apprehension of the overall shape. Clarification calls for simplifying, and one cannot simplify without disregarding and leaving out much of interest and value. Since one of the principal aims of this research is to discover where men join in agreeing about justice, one must prescind from the individualizing differences that distinguish one theory from another. The only differences taken into account are those that give rise to serious and fundamental disagreement—the issues, in short, that serve to isolate and locate the few major and basic positions regarding the nature of justice.

THE MEANING OF JUSTICE

It is not justice itself but theories about justice that constitute the object of investigation. But this description is still too broad. A theory of justice may cover much territory and include many topics and subtopics. Its range is vast in that justice is taken often as a kind of umbrella topic covering a wide variety of problems and considerations. For our purposes, however, all this diversity is out-of-bounds, as it were, and it enters, when it does, only incidentally for the light it throws on the meaning of the idea of justice.

The sole object of concern in this work is the idea of justice, that is to say, what idea men have of justice, what they say justice is or consists in, and even how they verbally define it, implicitly if not explicitly. The aim is to analyze the meaning of justice as it is found in the controversy about justice. It is to discover how a writer on justice would answer the question—What does it mean to say that X is just or unjust?

The problem of meaning is notorious for its treachery, and the question arises whether the search for the meaning of justice, even if only in the words men have written about it, is not an impossible task.

Good and learned men, seriously concerned about justice, have dismissed the search for the meaning of justice as a hopeless task and a waste of time and effort. Here, at the start, it is useful to consider these charges and show reason for believing that they can at least be circumvented.

Karl Popper declares, for example, that justice is always used in various senses, so that to ask for its meaning is to raise "an unimportant verbal question to which no definite answer can be given."[2] Charles L. Stevenson, too, warns against trying to find any one definite meaning: "The boundaries for the 'natural' meanings that may be assigned to 'good' (or 'just'), as is true of any vague term, are so shadowy and unstable that it is difficult to specify them even in a rough way. And there would be little gain if this were done; for confusions arise not from inattention to the boundaries, but from inattention to the many possible senses that lie between them."[3]

Yet Stevenson does not assert that there is no point at all in trying to differentiate among the different meanings. He explicitly allows that "the problem itself (and this is particularly true for 'justice') is an interesting and legitimate one when properly conceived." He even provides, at least in outline, the elements of what he considers a properly conceived analysis of justice. In the first place, "there must be no thought, in defining such a term as 'justice', of finding 'the' quality which people have always meant by the term, though perhaps implicitly and vaguely . . . So far as common usage is concerned, an analyst can do no more than indicate a *range* of meanings to which the term is susceptible." Furthermore, even in attempting to indicate the range of senses, "there must be no hope of a definitive treatment." Precision is impossible. The most that can be done consists either in "exemplifying numerous definitions and typical contexts . . . [or] in a more general manner—mentioning that the senses of justice have 'something to do' with the distribution of commodities or opportunities, or with equality, or with law, and so on." In either case, he claims "there is not always a uniform direction in the force that these considerations exert upon the term; and in the end one must acknowledge that the senses have only (in Wittgenstein's phrase) a family resemblance." Once the range of the meaning of the term has been shown and its emotive meaning taken into account, then, according to

2 *The Open Society and Its Enemies*, Vol. I, p. 89.
3 *Ethics and Language*, p. 208.

Stevenson, "the clarificatory aspects of the problem are virtually ended."[4]

Stevenson is concerned with justice itself and not with what men say about it. Yet his contention, like Popper's, has a direct bearing on our undertaking since both would seem to rule out the search for any unitary and definite meaning of justice as unrewarding, if not actually impossible. There are good reasons, however, for believing that their restrictions are overdrawn and that there is greater agreement about the meaning of justice than they would appear to allow.

THE COMMON SUBJECT OF CONTROVERSY

This becomes clear once we undertake to establish the common subject of controversy underlying the disagreement over justice. Without a common subject, no disagreement is possible, since the participants in the discussion are in that case talking about different things. Most arguments about justice arise over human actions and concern not meaning, but application. In such questions as whether or not the war in Vietnam is just or whether the Negro race has been treated unjustly there is no difficulty in identifying the subject of discussion. It is a certain war in one case and race relations in the other. But what sense does it make to ask for the common subject underlying the controversy over the meaning of justice? As a common subject, it must have certain characteristics that are accepted by all. Yet, as giving rise to controversy, men must have different things to say about it. A subject of controversy, in other words, must involve both agreement and disagreement.

This double condition serves at once to greatly lessen the diversity of the meanings of "justice" with which we have to deal. Much of the diversity is irrelevant in that it does not give rise to different interpretations and hence is not a subject of controversy. This limitation eliminates immediately, for example, all the adverbial uses of "just" noted above. Differences of opinion may arise over whether or not the wife did arrive when her husband was "just at the point of death," but the difference concerns a point of fact, not the adverbial meaning of "just."

To locate a common subject of justice that also involves disagreement, we need only consider some of the definitions that have been

[4] *Ibid.*, pp. 221–222.

offered of justice. For this purpose it is useful as well as of historical interest to consider the definitions occurring at the very beginning of the discussion about justice. They occur in the first great book on the subject of justice, which also contains the first record of the controversy over it, namely *The Republic* of Plato. This discussion can help us locate, identify, and delimit the subject of our investigation, and is therefore worth considering in some detail.

Socrates' search for justice is described as the search for a definition. In following the course of his hunt, we meet four different definitions, according as justice is defined as:

—telling the truth and rendering up what we have received (331c);
—rendering to each his due (331e);
—complying with the interest of the stronger, that is, of the ruling class as it is expressed in law (339a);
—minding one's own business both in external relations with others and in the internal ordering of the soul (434a; 443d).

As will be seen in the subsequent analysis of the literature, the second and third formulations represent perennial claimants as the best and most adequate definition of justice. The second is presented in *The Republic* as a quotation from the poet Simonides, and the third is that given by the power politician Thrasymachus. The fourth definition is the one finally offered by Socrates himself. At this point, the difference between them is not the primary concern. What we now want to see is how all of them suppose a common subject.

Very little consideration suffices to show that all four of the definitions share certain common assumptions about the meaning of justice. In addition to this, it can also be maintained that in the entire controversy about justice all the participants make the same assumptions. Whatever they may say about justice, however they may differ, all conceive of justice as having certain characteristics as a term or concept. These characteristics serve to identify justice as a common subject of controversy. Since they serve to make known the subject, they constitute common notes of the controversy.

Three such common notes can be distinguished. The first is that justice is a social norm, that is, a directive for guiding men in their actions toward one another. The second note is that justice is approbative in the sense that judging an action to be just manifests approval of that action. Third, justice is obligatory in that judging a certain course of action to be just entails that a person in the like situation ought to do the same thing.

JUSTICE IS A SOCIAL NORM

The four definitions given in *The Republic* agree in making justice a relational concept. It applies to a relation that supposes the existence of many terms. With one exception, which, however, is more apparent than real, all also assume that the relation in question is a social relation among men. Telling the truth, rendering to another what is due him, or obeying the law are all actions in which men are involved with other men. Justice, in all three, is conceived of as a guide by which men direct their actions in regard to others. It is not something that man has toward himself.

Socrates' own definition, especially in its second part, makes justice primarily a quality of the individual soul that has its various parts well ordered with respect to one another. It thus appears to be primarily a concept that applies to an individual and only derivatively a social concept. Yet it can be argued that the definition of justice in terms of the individual is more a matter of emphasis and a result of Plato's approach and analogical method than a denial that justice is primarily a social norm. *The Republic* seeks justice first in the state and only after it has been found there does the search turn to the individual. The justice of the soul, in other words, is known only after the pattern of justice is first seen in the state. Furthermore, Socrates himself maintains that doing injustice is worse than suffering it, and this presupposes that justice is social: by oneself one might be able to do injustice, but one could suffer it only at the hands of another. Socrates is led to define justice in terms of the interior ordering of the soul because of his desire to show why and how the doing of injustice harms the individual. In fact, he does not bring forth his own definition until he is challenged to show that justice is intrinsically good by the effects it has on its possessors (367e). He is thus led to emphasize justice as a virtue and a perfection of the soul scarcely distinguishable from that of all virtue. This, as will be seen is a characteristic tendency of one of the principal theories of justice as a social norm. Defining justice as an ordering of the soul rather than a regulating of our actions in regard to others is thus not the anomaly it first appears. Socrates in so doing might be considered as being primarily concerned with the source of justice in the soul and what it is that makes a man just in his action toward others.

When one turns to the literature on justice, one finds overwhelming evidence that justice is conceived of as a concept that applies to man in his social relations. It is assumed, when it is not stated explicitly, that justice occurs only where many men are gathered together in a social relationship. It is "a quality relating to men in society," Hobbes writes, "not in solitude."[5] Kelsen calls it "primarily a quality of the social order."[6] For Hume and the Utilitarian philosophers, justice is a "social virtue."[7] According to Aquinas, "justice lies in the *communicatio* that men have with each other"[8] and is "properly speaking, always concerned about things which are another's."[9] It is *ad alteram*, which leads Del Vecchio to say that *alteritas* is one of the basic elements of justice,[10] or, as it might be phrased, justice is other-directed.

Aristotle, apparently with Plato in mind, denies that, strictly speaking, there can be justice toward oneself, although he points out that it may be used metaphorically to indicate a similar relationship among the parts of the soul.[11] Aquinas also regards justice so considered as a metaphorical usage, and not the primary one.[12] But he notes that there are theological uses of this sort, notably the "original justice," of Adam and Eve in the garden and the state of soul of one who is "justified" by supernatural faith, both of which he interprets as the harmony in the interior dispositions of the soul whereby the lower is subject to the higher.[13]

Another feature apparent in Plato's account, which is borne out in the literature on justice, is the fact that justice is supposed as a condition and as an ideal, in some sense, by every society. It is not a quality like freedom, for instance, which may serve as an ideal for one society but not for another. Justice, John Rawls writes, is "supposed by every people, and societies differ, not in having or lacking it, but in the range of cases to which they apply it and the emphasis given to it

[5] *Leviathan*, p. 98.
[6] *The Metamorphoses of the Idea of Justice*, p. 390.
[7] *Enquiry Concerning the Principles of Morals*, p. 175.
[8] *In Decem Libros Ethicorum Aristotelis ad Nicomachum Expositio*, No. 1658.
[9] *Summa Theologica*, 2–2, 58, 1.
[10] *Op. cit.*, pp. 54, 70–72.
[11] See *Ethics*, 1138b7.
[12] See *op. cit.*, 2–2, 58, 2.
[13] See *ibid.*, 1–2, 113, 1; 2–2, 58, 2.

in relation to other moral concepts."[14] More briefly, in the words of Del Vecchio, *ubi societas, ibi jus,* that is, justice or right is found wherever society is.[15]

Saying that justice is a social norm sums up these various characteristics of justice accepted by all who discuss the subject: It is relational as involving many; it applies to men in association; and it is a norm for regulating their actions toward each other—that is, it is a directive.

Justice Is Approbative

There are still other features of justice, besides its being a social norm, which are admitted by all who discuss the subject. These are the features characterizing the kind of social norm that justice is taken to be. After all, society has more than one norm. There are norms of manners, of decency, of taste, of grammar, each of which provides a rule or guide for men in their association with one another, none of which is identical with the norm of justice. Justice is more closely associated with the norms of law or of morality. But whether or not justice is related to both law and morality, and how, are matters of disagreement and controversy. In fact, such questions will be seen to provide the issues that are most central to the whole controversy about justice. Thus little help in identifying the subject of the controversy is to be obtained from noting that justice is a legal or moral norm. There are two features about justice, however, which are admitted by all. These are most succinctly described by noting that justice as a social norm is both approbative and obligatory.

It is agreed in the literature about it that justice is a concept that is used for evaluating men and their actions. To say that X is just is to evaluate X as good; to say that X is unjust is to evaluate X as bad. Since the evaluation in terms of justice is always positive in that it shows approval, it can be said that justice is an approbative concept. "Justice," R. M. Hare writes, is "a word of commending, like 'good' " and is used to guide choices.[16] Sidgwick is representative of all when, in analyzing what he calls the common sense notion of justice, he declares that it is "a quality which it is ultimately desirable to realize in conduct and the social relations of men."[17]

---

[14] "Justice as Fairness" in Olafson, *Justice and Social Policies,* p. 107.
[15] *Op. cit.,* p. 114.
[16] *The Language of Morals,* p. 127.
[17] *Methods of Ethics,* p. 264.

In the literature, this much is usually assumed without explicit comment. The attempt is seldom made to show that if X is just it is also good, approved of, and praiseworthy. *The Republic,* however, is an exception. Thrasymachus is presented as arguing that justice as it is usually understood is the opposite of virtue and wisdom and, hence, is evil and folly (348E). For his part he proposes that justice is really nothing but "the interest of the stronger." Yet both his attack and his own definition, in fact, suppose that justice is approbative in character. The conventional justice that he attacks as weak and to be scorned is disapproved precisely because, in his view, it is a caricature of what justice really is. His own definition of what justice "really is" retains its approbative character since he considers it good and desirable that the interest of the stronger should prevail. The "disapprobative" character of justice as Thrasymachus presents it results from the extravagant and intentionally shocking language in which he has formulated his position. Glaucon's intervention emphasizes this point by taking up again the argument of Thrasymachus and giving it a social contract interpretation that removes the offensive character of the definition and reestablishes justice as enjoying the approbation of all by a sort of compromise (358B). He then challenges Socrates to prove that justice is absolutely better than injustice for the individual who practices it.

That justice is approbative is a common note of the subject. But men disagree about how this is to be understood and interpreted. All would agree that to say that X is just is to indicate a "pro attitude" toward X. Justice is thus recognized as belonging to the realm of value and hence also involves the emotions or the emotional side of man. "Nobody in their senses could fail to know," A. C. Ewing writes, "that ethical judgments have a practical emotive function."[18] That justice involves attitudes and feelings is admitted throughout the controversy. But whether the approbative feature of justice is any more than this, whether it also rests on an objective judgment, is matter for dispute.

JUSTICE IS OBLIGATORY

To say that X is a just action is to do more than merely to indicate that X has been evaluated as good and meets with the approval of the speaker or his society. The statement also entails that X ought to be done when one is in a like situation. Besides being evaluative, justice

[18] *Ethics,* p. 88.

is also obligatory or prescriptive. Unlike norms of manners or grammar, justice is a social norm that imposes an obligation or duty on the members of the society. The just thing to do in a given situation is what one ought to do, and not to do it is to be, to that extent, unjust.

All theories of justice agree that justice involves in some way a norm or standard of what ought to be done. They differ, however, about the nature and ground of the norm and how and why it obliges. Some assert the existence of a distinctly moral *ought* that imposes an unconditional obligation, while others deny it. But none deny, however they may explain it, that justice imposes an obligation.

Not all writers say so explicitly or in these very words. In some, it is assumed and taken for granted. In others it appears in the analysis of the duties and obligations of justice. *The Republic* says little about obligation as such, yet the whole book is in one sense an elaborate justification of why one ought to be just. Recent analytical accounts of the concept of justice describe its obligatory character in a variety of ways. George H. von Wright distinguishes what he calls the normative from the evaluative character of justice, corresponding respectively to what we have termed the obligatory and the approbative note.[19] Hare says that justice involves a "value-judgment," but, by this means, that it is "an action-guiding statement that entails an imperative," thus making it equivalent to an obligatory norm.[20] Both Alf Ross[21] and P. de Tourtoulon[22] describe justice as a "directive" for action. Carl Wellman[23] speaks of statements of obligation as having "critical meaning." Stevenson develops a theory of what he calls "persuasive definitions," and claims that the appeal to justice involves an attempt to persuade others to adopt a certain attitude and course of action.[24] But under this diversity of language, it is clear that each is asserting that justice is a social norm that is both approbative and obligatory.

THE COMMON NOTES OF JUSTICE

The three notes of justice provide, as it were, the data accepted and agreed to by all in the controversy. However justice may be interpreted, and whatever else it may be, it is acknowledged to oblige us to

[19] See *The Varieties of Goodness*, p. 7.
[20] *Op. cit.*, pp. 167–169.
[21] See *On Law and Justice*, pp. 7–8.
[22] See *Philosophy in the Development of Law*, p. 51.
[23] See *The Language of Ethics*, p. 270.
[24] See *op. cit.*, p. 220; see also *Persuasive Definitions*, pp. 342–344.

do something that concerns another, the performance of which elicits approval. Other terms and topics occur widely and commonly in discussions about justice. Matters involving law, social utility, and right give rise to judgments in terms of justice. Questions of justice and injustice also arise in matters concerning exchange and distribution, in which the analysis frequently involves appeal to things such as equality and inequality, property, and desert, or merit. In the discussion of justice, however, there is a crucial difference between the two sets of terms—that is, between the three notes that have been distinguished and all the terms just enumerated. As will be seen when we come to analyze the various theories, these other terms figure in the explanations that are offered of the way in which justice is an approbative, obligatory, social norm. In other words, terms such as "right," "law," and "equality" are part of the theories, and in different theories they differ in importance and significance and in the way they are related to the other terms comprising the account that is given of the subject identified by the three common notes.

The three common notes enable us to identify a common subject of controversy, and the agreement about them assures us that those engaged in discussing the nature of justice are talking about the same thing. Disagreement and controversy begin when we go on to demand further specification of the norm of justice and explanation of how and why it obliges and elicits approval. What is the norm of justice and on what is it based? Why does, why should justice and the doing of a just act elicit our approval? Why does justice oblige us to the performance of its dictates? These questions about the common notes of justice generate issues over which controversy arises. They receive different answers that lead to different theories of justice.

The three common notes of justice have been obtained from the literature on the subject, that is from what men have to say about justice. They are, one may say, a dialectical discovery. The question then arises whether the three notes apply to justice itself and not merely to the literature on it; whether, in other words, justice is uniquely determined as being an approbative, obligatory, social norm. The question is a difficult one, and it is philosophical, not dialectical, hence out-of-bounds. I would remark, however, that the three notes do seem to distinguish justice from those terms with which it is most nearly associated in the literature, that is, from law, benevolence, and the moral good or right. The note of being approbative serves to distinguish justice from law, for although law may constitute an obligatory social norm, it obviously does not always enjoy the approval of those within its jurisdiction. Benevolence is a social virtue, but not all would agree that it is a duty incumbent upon all men in the same way that justice is. The moral good or right is wider and less specific than justice, since, at least according to some theories, it is not always social—the determination of such a good as temperance or courage being relative to the individual and not to any definitely established social norm. Only justice, of all of these notions, implies a norm that is at one and the same time approbative, obligatory, and social.

For the purposes of our investigation, however, this question can be put to one side. Whether or not the three notes uniquely determine the concept of justice in itself, they do provide an analytical means for clarifying the controversy over justice. They not only identify a common subject but they also provide a simple and ready way to narrow the discussion of it so as to clarify the shape and structure of the controversy. In turning to the extensive literature, we direct our attention in the analysis of any theory of justice solely to the account that it can offer of justice as an approbative, obligatory, social norm. Concentrating on the idea of justice in these respects at once effects a drastic reduction in the vast range of matters that are treated in the major treatises on justice. Little or no need will arise for considering in the concrete what is the just thing to do in such and such circumstances, or the rights and duties of men in their various offices and of their conflict and just resolution. We need pay little attention to the various kinds of justice and injustice, of murder, theft, and robbery, of judicial procedures, of economic justice in buying and selling and lending and borrowing, or of the kinds of respect we owe to others, to God, our fellowmen, and our family.

Narrowing the subject as indicated eliminates from consideration still other topics frequently discussed in theories of justice. Concentrating on justice as a social norm, and how it regulates our actions toward others, offers little occasion to consider justice in the moral life, its relation to other virtues, and its place among them—whether, for instance, it is the highest virtue. There is likewise little place for discussion of the possibility of justice, and whether, as H. J. Morgenthau claims, for example, man is so limited that the achievement of justice is impossible;[25] or, as Augustine claims, that it is possible only

[25] See *On Trying to be Just,* p. 422.

in God.[26] So, too, there is no need to consider even the more important uses of justice, and to trace, for example, the conditions that have to be satisfied to warrant speaking of a just government, a just state, a just war, or a just international society. Even the topic of the limits of justice and the need for tempering justice with equity or love and mercy finds no place in our analysis.

The historical dimension of justice also lies outside the scope of our investigation. Man's understanding of justice, and of what is just or unjust, changes and develops through the course of time and differs in different cultures and civilizations. The enslavement of men and the subjection of women were once thought to be in no way unjust. Such examples could readily be multiplied. Yet there is no need, since it is immediately clear that any justification of them would involve appeal to a social norm defended as good. The question defining our investigation is not whether or not slavery is just, but rather what it would mean to make the claim one way or the other. And the answer to this question is apparent once we see how justice is specified and understood as an approbative, obligatory, social norm.

The limitations within which the investigation has been carried out are scarcely more stringent than that characteristic of much recent ethical and philosophical work. This is frequently restricted to the analysis of a concept and its various uses, or to what J. L. Austin once called "the phenomenological analysis of language." In the scope of its concern, this work is closer to such an approach than it is to the treatment of justice in the grand manner characteristic of Plato and Aristotle, Aquinas and Suarez, Bentham, and even Sidgwick. Nonetheless, a fundamental difference remains. It lies in the fact that the work aims only at a dialectical clarification of the controversy about justice and not at a philosophical analysis and clarification of justice. The idea of justice, which is the object of our investigation, is the idea of it that is to be found in the various theories that men have elaborated about justice, and not the concept of justice as it is used by men in the work of the world. The material of our study is provided by what men have said about justice when they have consciously posed it as a problem demanding analysis and illumination. But we have approached it only to find out how they would account for justice as a norm that is approbative, obligatory, and social.

The three notes, as already indicated, may well be the identifying

[26] See *The City of God*, xix. 4.

marks of justice itself as it is used as a concept, outside of theories about it. But whether they are or not is a philosophical question, and the investigating and testing of it would demand a thorough inventory and classification of the various appearances and uses of justice. That is an interesting and important task, but it is not the task undertaken in this book. Here the three common notes that have been found in the discussion of justice have been used, not as the basis for pursuing a philosophical investigation into the nature of justice, but as a means or device for clarifying the theoretical discussion men have had about it. The measure of their success lies in their ability to make better sense out of much confusing and conflicting discussion, and this can be judged only after we have obtained the result.

2

The Fundamental Issues
of the Controversy

THE three notes of justice provide a common subject of controversy—a subject, that is, about which many authors have written and about which they disagree. They agree about these notes of
justice—that is, they admit that justice is an approbative, obligatory,
social norm in the sense that has been indicated in the previous chapter.
But they disagree in what they have to say about these various notes of
justice and how they explain each one and relate them together in
their account of justice.

There are many theories of justice, in fact, as many as there are
writers on the subject, since any one writer departs in some respect
from what others have said about it. Yet all the theories are not
equally close or remote from one another. They tend to fall into more
or less definitely marked groups. The theories of Kelsen and Hobbes,
for instance, are closer each other than either is to that of Aristotle.
But to make this judgment and substantiate it we need questions that
all three authors face and to which they offer answers that can be
compared. We need questions that pose issues on which different
positions can be taken.

The kind of questions and issues that we need is clear from our purpose. We want to make better sense out of the controversy regarding justice by locating, identifying, and comparing the major sources of agreement and disagreement among the various theories. For this purpose not all the questions discussed in the literature about justice are equally useful. One author may consider an idea or topic essential to the analysis of justice while other authors pay no attention to it at all. Such is the notion of freedom in Hegel's analysis of justice and that of spirit or consciousness in Del Vecchio's account. Although these ideas could be used to formulate issues which would serve to distinguish these authors and their followers from others, they would do little more than this. They would not distinguish basic positions regarding justice, capable of accommodating many philosophers of different persuasions. They would not simplify and clarify the controversy by reducing the large number of diverse theories to a few well marked basic positions. Such issues may be philosophically fundamental for their authors, and even illuminating for the understanding of justice, but they are not dialectically fundamental. To satisfy this requirement they must be issues that constitute common issues of the whole controversy—questions, that is, which all the participants consider, implicitly or explicitly, and on which they take a determinable position.

The three common notes of justice that we have discovered in the literature provide a means of constructing issues that are dialectically fundamental. From them we can generate issues that are considered by all the authors. Stated as questions, they elicit answers in which each author asserts a definite position. The positions on each of the issues taken together constitute an author's theory of justice with respect to its common notes. The theory so formulated will not comprise any author's complete theory of justice, since any writer discusses more than the character of justice as an approbative, obligatory, social norm. Yet the formulation that we obtain will constitute an important and fundamental part of his theory, since it will reveal how he construes the meaning of justice with respect to the very notes that all theories of justice take to be common.

Many differences can be found among the various theories of justice. Some authors approach the subject in a special way that is all their own and elaborate a special terminology for talking about it. Some of them develop a theory of justice only as part of a vast philosophical system. But all, for the most part, in writing about justice address themselves in one way or another to each of the small number of issues that are dialectically fundamental. Many explicitly, in so many words, adopt a definite position on a given issue. But even when they do not, it is usually possible from what they do say on other matters to see what position they would take were the question addressed to them. Their position on these issues is implicit in what they have to say about other aspects of justice and can be made explicit without misinterpreting their theory. Admittedly, there are a few authors—Plato and Hegel being perhaps the most notorious in this respect—who seem to resist taking a definite position on the very issues that serve to divide most others. Their whole theory often seems designed to avoid such questions in an attempt to encompass what others take to be opposite answers. They are the dialectically difficult authors who resist classification and cannot be identified exclusively with any one group, except with great qualification.

Except for these authors, and they are not many, most writers on justice take a definite position on the issues that are dialectically fundamental. The position taken with respect to these issues provides the means of identifying and comparing the different theories of justice, and the resulting pattern of agreements and disagreements provides an index or key to the major families. In short, these fundamental issues comprise the questions that have been found to be the most useful for analyzing and classifying the various theories of justice. They provide a taxonomic key to the vast literature dealing with justice.

THE FUNDAMENTAL ISSUES

F1. Is justice the same as legality?

F2. Is justice a criterion of law?

F3. Is justice based on natural right?

F4. Is justice, in any sense other than that of legality, an objective norm of human action?

F5. Is justice obligatory on its own, apart from legal or social sanctions?

F6. Is justice a distinct virtue?

We have stated six fundamental issues. But we had only three common notes, from which we claim the issues are derived. Why then six issues and only three notes, and what is their relation? The rest of the chapter will be devoted to answering these questions. But first it may be useful to say something about the way in which the issues are formulated and show how they can fulfill their dialectical role of differentiating one theory from another.

In most cases the wording of the issue shows its dependence upon the common note from which it derives. Thus the first four issues bear in different ways upon justice as a norm: whether it is to be identified with law, that is, with positive, man-made law; whether it is based on natural right; and whether or not it is objective. The fifth issue concerns the obligatory character of justice and why the just act ought to be done. The remaining common datum—justice being an approbative concept—is dealt with not only in connection with the sixth issue concerning justice as a virtue but also with the fourth on the objectivity of justice.

The precise terms in which the issues are formulated, as well as their order of presentation, are to some extent a matter of choice and convenience. The test that any formulation has to meet is that of identifying and classifying the various theories of justice, and the one given above passes that test. The issues as formulated raise questions that most theories answer definitely in one way or another. They also cut down the number of basically different theories to a very small number.

Each issue is formulated in a question that elicits a "yes" or "no" answer so as to provide a dichotomous principle of classification. Some of the issues are interrelated, so that taking a definite position on one entails a definite position on the others. As a result, it is possible to obtain different combinations of affirmatives and negatives to the various questions. These differing patterns serve to identify and characterize the basic positions among the many theories of justice.

There are only three basic positions in the controversy about justice. One, which I call the Positive Law theory, identifies justice with conformity to positive law. It answers the first question in the affirmative and all the remaining ones in the negative. The other two basic positions deny that justice can be identified with obeying the law, and they affirm, on the contrary, that justice is also a criterion of law. But they part company on the third issue regarding the naturalness of justice. One claims that justice is based on natural right, and it is accordingly called the Natural Right theory of justice. The third basic position is so far characterized only negatively as denying both that justice is identical with legality and that it is based on natural right. Positively, it is characterized by the claim that justice consists fundamentally in promoting the social good, and I accordingly call it the Social Good theory of justice.

The fact that we must go beyond the terms of the issues to obtain the identifying note of the Social Good theory reveals what latitude there is in their formulation. Why, it might be asked, should the privileged terms of the other two theories appear in the formulation of the issues while that of the Social Good theory is left out? Issues could be formulated in terms of this theory that would serve to discriminate it from the other two, and these could be added to the list or replace some of the others.

Little would be gained by such a change, however, and it has seemed preferable, because simpler and clearer, to keep the issues as formulated. Of the three basic positions, the Positive Law theory and the Natural Right theory are the extremes. The one takes the affirmative position on the first issue and the negative on the other five issues, whereas the other theory takes the negative position on the first and the affirmative on the remaining five. The Social Good position falls in between these two extremes in that it takes the negative on the first and third issue and the affirmative on the remainder.

Both the Social Good theory and the Natural Right theory join in common opposition to the Positive Law theory in taking the affirmative position on the issues regarding objectivity, obligation, and virtue. Yet this agreement is more apparent than real and arises from the way in which the issues have been formulated so as to yield a dichotomous division. Once the position of the two theories on these issues is investigated, it becomes evident that the differences between them are considerable and deep. But this consideration will have to wait until after the detailed analysis and exposition of the two theories.

Before turning to that task, still more remains to be said about the issues in relation to the common notes and how they can be used to draw up a plan for analyzing and clarifying the controversy. Consideration of each particular issue will also provide occasion for noting, at least in a preliminary way, the difference between the basic theories.

ISSUES REGARDING THE SOCIAL NORM

All theories agree that justice is a social norm. It supplies a guide or directive by which men can regulate their actions toward their fellow-men. The just thing is what one ought to do, the unjust thing what ought to be avoided. Justice is thus frequently spoken of as a norm, a standard, a criterion, or measure by which men may judge and evaluate human acts.

Differences about the normative character of justice do not begin to appear until one goes on to ask for its specification, its source or basis, and actual content. To such questions as these, different theories give different and divergent answers, which reveal different conceptions, not only of the content of the norm but also of the norm itself, its function, and how specific it should be.

All theories of justice would agree that what is just is sometimes identical with what is legal or lawful and that the man who breaks the law is to that extent unjust. Cases occur in which a person can deny that he did anything unjust and support his claim by arguing that he has violated no law. There is also some evidence that in the ordinary course of things we usually come to learn about justice and injustice through their connection with the law and with keeping or violating it. Piaget reports that children acquire their first notion of justice from the ideas of duty and obedience to the commands of adult authority, which leads him to assert that what is just is first known as "what is imposed by law."

This much would be generally admitted. But some theories go still further and maintain that this situation also indicates where the basic meaning of justice is to be found. Justice in the most important sense of the term is then identified with conformity to law.

It must be noted and emphasized at once that the only law in question is the positive law of man's own making in organized society—the law of the land. No other law, either natural law or God's law, is intended or implied, and any such implication is now and henceforth for the whole of our investigation set aside. Whenever any mention of law is made, it refers only to the positive law, unless clearly stipulated otherwise.

The reason for such a stipulation is simple. As we shall see, many theories claim that justice depends upon law, but mean by this not the positive law made by men but the natural law or some higher law, which they then appeal to as a norm not only for man's actions but also for his positive laws. Whether or not there exists such a law is a matter of dispute, but it is a dispute about law, not about justice, and what relevance it does have to questions about justice can be handled in other ways, as will be seen.

Furthermore, for our purposes there is no need to raise the immense question of natural law, and one can avoid doing so by a simple logical distinction. Nobody denies the existence of positive law as a norm by which men regulate their affairs. Suppose we now ask of this positive law, whether justice depends upon law and also whether justice is itself a criterion of law. Speaking merely logically, it is impossible to answer both questions in the affirmative without using law in two different senses. The law cannot in both cases be merely positive law. If positive law is determinative of justice, then to hold that justice is a criterion of law is to maintain that positive law is its own criterion, which either destroys the notion of criterion altogether or reduces to the trivial statement that a law is a law. Put conversely, this is to say that if justice is a criterion of law, then that law, understood in the same sense, cannot also be determinative of justice. A criterion or measure and that which it measures belong logically to different orders. Hence those who do maintain that justice supposes law and then go on to claim that justice is also a criterion of law must be using law in two different senses—the law in the second sense usually being identified with natural law.

To use law in these two different senses—positive and natural— would cause great confusion in analyzing the various theories of justice. It would also involve discussions about the nature of law not immediately relevant to the theory of justice. We can avoid these difficulties by restricting the word "law," as used in this book, to refer only to positive, man-made law.

It has already become evident that questions about law pose fundamental issues that serve to discriminate among the various theories of justice. We obtain different answers to such questions as the following: Does it make sense to raise questions of justice and injustice in matters where there is no law and where there should not be any law? How about law itself? Can a law be just or unjust? In other words, is justice a criterion of law? These questions yield the first two fundamental issues—F1–F2.

Such questions as these elicit different answers and reveal different theories of justice. Disagreement about them also indicates that the initial agreement that the just sometimes consists in the lawful is itself superficial. This proposition is understood differently, depending on how the law is considered to be related to justice. For some theories, the only objective and determinate meaning of justice is conformity to the law. For them, to be just means to act so as to conform to the law. But on other theories the lawful is the just only if the law itself is just, and, conceivably, cases could arise in which the only just course of action would consist in disobeying the law.

Thus it is clear that there is an issue regarding law that divides all theories of justice into two groups. On one side are those theories that maintain that justice is fundamentally the same as lawfulness or legality; that to be just consists in doing what is in conformity to the law; and that the law, as the standard or norm of justice, is not itself just or unjust. Such is the Positive Law position on justice.

On the other side are the theories that deny that justice can be equated with legality. They maintain that there are questions and occasions outside the reach of law where it makes good sense to speak of justice and injustice. They hold also that law itself can be measured by justice, that justice, then, is a criterion of the goodness of law.

The issues with regard to law identify positively one of the three basic positions on justice, that is, the Positive Law theory. They identify only negatively, however, those other theories that hold that justice is wider than law and legality. For positive characterization of these theories we must turn to other issues concerning justice.

One of the major sources of contention since the very beginning of the controversy has been over the question whether justice is natural or conventional. If justice is only a matter of positive law, it is entirely conventional in the sense that it results from the agreement and decision of men in society; it is man made. Such a view of the conventional basis of justice is highly legalistic, and it is not necessary to identify the conventional so strictly with the explicitly legal. One may maintain that justice is still conventional by claiming that justice is produced by and in society and depends exclusively upon it and has no natural basis. Social contract theories of the origin of society and of law often take such a position and maintain in effect that society and its needs give rise to both law and justice. The legalistic version, on the other hand, tends to make law itself productive of society as well as of justice. Both positions, however, are conventional in denying that justice has any natural basis.

No theory of justice would deny that questions of justice and injustice may concern matters of conventional agreement among men in society—how they may best distribute their burdens and rewards, what is fair treatment in their common life, and the like. Disagreement does arise, however, when we ask whether justice is ever anything more than conventional, whether it has a natural basis apart from convention or agreement, and whether it makes sense to think of justice apart from leading a common life in organized society.

The question of natural right thus provides us with a fundamental issue, namely F3. In asking whether justice is based on natural right, it raises the question whether justice as a social norm has a natural basis. The issue is phrased in terms of right, which is a subject on which all theories of justice have something to say, and it asks whether the rights men have are entirely and exclusively conferred by society or whether they also have a natural basis. So understood, this issue serves to divide all theories of justice into two groups: those who deny and those who affirm that justice is based on natural right. The affirmative position identifies the Natural Right theory of justice. It includes the theories that base justice on natural law, although, as we shall see, some theories adopt the Natural Right theory of justice without asserting the existence of natural law. But this is only to note that men may differ about natural law and still agree that justice is in some sense natural and is not entirely conventional.

The negative position on this issue, combined with the denial that justice is identical with legality, serves to identify still another basic position, which is opposed to both the other two. This theory is positively identified by the assertion that the social good, and neither law nor natural right, is the basic term for the analysis of justice and accordingly provides the basic proposition of the Social Good theory of justice.

Natural right, like law, provides an issue that divides all theories of justice into two groups. But the two issues do not make the same cut among the theories of justice; they do not yield the same groups. The issue regarding law serves to locate the proponents of the Positive Law theory on one side and to leave the proponents of both the Natural Right and the Social Good theories on the other side. The issue of natural right serves to isolate the Natural Right authors, and groups together both Positive Law and Social Good authors.

The way the two issues make different cuts among the theories of justice and yield different groupings can be shown by stating positively the positions that can be taken. Thus, on the issue regarding legality, we have the position summarized in the following proposition:

(1) The laws made by a state or government are the only directions of conduct applying to men in society that establish a norm of justice.

The affirmative assertion of this proposition is the identifying note of the Positive Law theory of justice. It is denied by both the Social Good and the Natural Right theories.

On the issue of natural right, we can formulate a position that denies it in terms of the relation between justice and society, as follows:

(2) The rights of man and rules of justice based on them are conferred by society and are exclusively the result of man's efforts to achieve a viable and good social life.

The affirmative assertion of this proposition, amounting to a denial of natural right, is shared by both the Positive Law and the Social Good theories of justice. The denial of it characterizes the Natural Right position, which is asserted positively by the claim that natural right provides a basis for justice.

In this issue, nature is obviously the important and identifying note. Yet the mere use of the word "nature," or one of its cognates, in the analysis of justice does not suffice to make one an adherent of the Natural Right theory. In fact, authors who use the term can be found among all three of the basic theories. Hobbes talks of natural laws, and Hume speaks of natural justice. Yet neither of them belongs in the group of Natural Right authors, as we use the term to designate a basic position concerning the meaning of justice; Hobbes subscribes to the Positive Law Theory and Hume to the Social Good theory. The presence of the terms "nature," "natural law," or "natural right" in a theory of justice does not by itself identify an adherent of the Natural Right position. The denial of natural right, however, does serve to identify a non-Natural Right author, as does the denial that nature has anything to do with justice.

The issues concerning law and natural right elicit answers that reveal the basically different positions taken with regard to justice as a social norm. One identifies that norm with the positive law; another maintains that natural right provides a basis for the norm of justice; the third, falling as it were in between these two, holds that justice is a norm established by society for the social good, which supplies a criterion for law, hence is not identical with it, yet is not based on natural right. The difference between the three becomes still more pronounced as we proceed to consider the other fundamental issues.

THE ISSUE REGARDING APPROBATIVENESS

All theories of justice admit, as a common datum, that to declare that X is just is thereby to indicate approval of X. Justice is an approbative concept, and this much is admitted by the Positive Law theory as well as by the two others. It differs from them, however, in separating the approbative character of justice from its normative character. According to this theory, to say that X is just and mean by it anything other than that X conforms to the law of the land is to say nothing more than that one individually approves of X. Such a statement has no objective meaning and says nothing about X, but only indicates the attitude of the speaker toward it. On the Positive Law theory, justice apart from legality is never anything more than a manifestation of subjective approval.

Proponents of the other two theories admit that justice is approbative, but deny that it is merely subjective. They maintain that "X is just" is a judgment that one may make of law itself as well as of matters on which there is no law, and that in addition to manifesting the speaker's attitude toward X, it also makes an objective assertion about X. Both the Social Good and the Natural Right authors join in common opposition to the Positive Law position in maintaining that justice has an objective basis apart from law.

They part, however, and disagree about the basis of this objectivity. The one theory holds that the social good provides an objective basis, whereas the other identifies this basis with natural right founded on the nature of man. Thus the one interprets the judgment that X is just as making an objective statement about X in relation to the social good and holds that it is something that is approved of for this very reason. The other theory allows that there may be cases in which the social good provides the basis, but, in addition to this, it also claims that cases may arise in which the social good is not implicated at all. That X is just in this case means that X is something objectively due to another because he is a man, and the approval of it is rooted in this very fact and no other. There is no need to appeal to law or to social good, since what is involved is a matter of what is naturally due to another as a matter of right.

The Social Good and the Natural Right theories agree that justice is objective, but they disagree about its basis since they disagree about the norm of justice. According to the Positive Law theory, the whole normative character of justice insofar as it has any objective meaning at all is expounded in the statement that X is in accord with the law. The other two theories agree that there may be cases in which this holds true, but they maintain that this does not exhaust the meaning of justice. "X is just" may still have an objective meaning different from this one of legality. But, for the one theory, this objective meaning is manifested in the statement that X is something that preserves and promotes the social good, whereas, on the other theory, it is held that X is based on or is a matter of natural right.

If one now goes on to ask why, in judging that X is just, does one also indicate his approval of X, the two latter theories answer that approval is, as it were, built into the norm, since it is natural and normal for men to approve of what is for the social good or based on natural right. The Positive Law theory does not always have this recourse, since law and approval of it do not always coincide, and the approbative character is accordingly held to be an entirely subjective judgment relative to the individual.

The issue of objectivity, expressed in F4, thus serves to reveal the disagreements among the theories regarding the approbative character of justice. As in the case of justice as a social norm, there is no disagreement with respect to the note itself: all the theories grant that justice is both approbative and a social norm. But they disagree with regard to the impact or significance of those common data and how they are to be explained and related together to account for justice. The common notes are separately distinct, but they are related differently by different theories.

THE ISSUE REGARDING OBLIGATORINESS

All the theories agree that justice involves obligation and imposes a duty. One ought to do the just thing and refrain from doing the unjust thing; one ought to be just. But why ought one be just? This question elicits different answers from the three different theories that have been distinguished. The Natural Right theory tends to take the position that one ought to be just and do the just act for no other reason than that it is just. Justice supplies its own sanction, and no other is absolutely necessary. Whether or not society imposes sanctions so as to guarantee that justice is done is a separate question and dependent upon the circumstances. The *ought* of justice has in itself an unconditional and moral obligation.

The answer of the other two theories is more complex, since each looks beyond justice itself for a reason to explain the duty it imposes. For them, the *ought* of justice thus is not unconditional and categorical but hypothetical. But we need to distinguish three different kinds of hypothetical *oughts* to clearly differentiate their answers. For this purpose it is useful to distinguish what may be called the penal, the approbative, and the teleological *ought*. All are hypothetical in that they can take the form of a conditional statement such as: "You ought to do X if you want to avoid——." The three kinds of hypothetical *oughts* can then be distinguished by the term that fills the last blank, according as the evil to be avoided is pain, disapproval, or failure.

For the Positive Law theory, the *ought* of justice tends to be identified with the penal or the approbative *ought,* while for the Social Good theory it is teleological. The Positive Law answer is two-part, depending on whether justice is being used in an objective or a subjective sense. If objective, justice is identical with conformity to law and one ought to be just for the same reason that one ought to obey the law, which is ultimately in order to avoid punishment. If justice is used subjectively, it rests on a subjective judgment of approval, and the *ought* involved is merely approbative: one ought to be just because that is what is approved of.

The answer of the Social Good theory is less clear, since some of its adherents come very close to the Natural Right answer, while others approach the Positive Law position. Where it differs from both lies in its insistence that the good of society provides the ultimate sanction. One must be just in order to achieve the social good. Justice then is looked upon as a means to the social good as an end, and the *ought* of justice is teleological.

Further light upon this position as well as upon the whole discussion of justice can be obtained from consideration of what has been called the "naturalist fallacy." This fallacy, because of its name, must not be associated exclusively with the Natural Right position. In fact, the Social Good writers would be most concerned about it. The fallacy, for our purposes, is best described as the fallacy of deriving an *ought* statement from premises consisting entirely of *is*-statements.

Thus the mere fact that a given course of action *is* socially good in some way does not of itself impose a duty. For that, we also need to know that what is social good *ought* to be done. Why the Social Good authors should be especially concerned is clear from their position regarding the *ought* of justice: One ought to be just because of the common good, they maintain; but why ought one to want and promote the common good? If the only reason is to avoid the sanctions of society, one is back in the Positive Law position, which is explicitly denied, on this very issue, by the Social Good authors. But if it is maintained that one ought to promote the common good as a moral obligation and a duty on its own, which contains within itself, as it were, its own moral force, the theory agrees with the Natural Right position in opposition to the Positive Law theory: justice is obligatory on its own and not merely because of the social and political sanctions with which it may be backed up.

THE ISSUE REGARDING VIRTUE

The five issues so far considered have accounted for all three of the common notes regarding justice. Yet one fundamental issue still remains. Expressed as it is in F6, asking whether justice is a distinct virtue, it seems to dangle without having any clear relevance to the others. It admittedly differs from the other issues, yet it still remains intimately connected with the common data. In a way it relates to all three of them, since, on one of the theories, all three characteristics of justice are explained by its being a distinct virtue. In fact, many of the Natural Right authors elaborate their theory of justice as part of a larger theory of virtue. Justice is presented as preeminently the social virtue establishing the norm for men in their association with one another, which is approved and should be obeyed precisely because its good is an intrinsic good or a virtuous good, a *bonum honestum.*

Only one of the three basic theories links its account of justice so closely to that of virtue. Yet it is still dialectically fruitful to pose the issue to the other theories. To do so is to inquire what kind of good justice is conceived to be as well as the kind of character that the just man possesses. The answers that are given reveal significant differences, which throw further light on the shape of the controversy as a whole.

On the Positive Law theory, justice reduces to obedience to the

law. Nothing more is demanded, since justice itself is identified with
legality. The other basic theories refuse to identify justice with
legality and claim that the virtue of justice implies something more
than mere obedience. Both theories agree that it is a distinct virtue,
but each position sees its distinctness in a different way.

The Social Good writers, unlike the proponents of the other two
theories, usually discuss justice in connection with benevolence. Although they hold that the two are distinct, they feel some tendency to
assimilate them to each other, since both are social virtues and have
the common good or social utility as their end.

The Natural Right theory does not have this difficulty. When
Natural Right writers discuss justice along with the other virtues, it is
usually in connection with the cardinal virtues, and not with benevolence. Yet the theory is like the Social Good theory in having its own
difficulty in discussing justice as a virtue. The difficulty appears in the
ambiguity of "right" as the object of justice and yet as also coextensive
with the moral good. Thus, within the Natural Right position, the
tendency is sometimes felt to identify justice with the whole of virtue.
The tendency is most evident in *The Republic* of Plato, where often
it is the moral good as such, and not a particular form of it, that is the
main concern.

The fact that the discussion of justice as a virtue falls within a
different context in each theory shows that the issue regarding virtue
is dialectically fundamental. It serves to distinguish one theory from
another.

We have now completed our account of the six fundamental issues
and have shown how they can be generated from the three common
data regarding justice accepted by all theories. In doing so, we have
seen in a preliminary way how the issues serve to distinguish and
identify the few basic theories regarding the meaning of justice. The
positions taken on the six issues serve, in a summary way, to identify a
basic theory. Thus the Positive Law theory of justice is characterized
by the following propositions, which assert its position on the six
fundamental issues:

(1) Justice is the same as legality.
(2) Justice is not a criterion of law.
(3) Justice is not based on natural right.
(4) Justice, apart from legality, is merely a subjective norm.

(5) Justice is obligatory ultimately only because of legal and political sanctions.

(6) Justice as a virtue is identical with obedience.

Of course, such a list of identifying propositions provides the merest sketch of a theory of justice, and until we see how each of the propositions is developed and explained, we cannot understand much about it. Once that is done, not only for this one theory but for all three of the basic ones, we will be in the position to compare them with each other, to locate their agreements and disagreements, and hence to understand better the shape of the controversy as a whole.

II

The
Basic Theories
of Justice

3

Plan of Analysis

THE fundamental issues provide us with the means for analyzing a theory of justice so as to reveal its agreement and disagreement with other theories. By applying them to the literature, we have identified and distinguished three basic theories of the subject. But, so far, we have seen only the most schematic description of any of these theories. To fill out that description and provide a detailed analysis of each of the three theories is the task of this part, consisting of the next three chapters.

In the exposition and elucidation of the basic theories, I have two main aims. First, to present each theory so that it can be seen and judged for itself and on its own, but also in such a way that its agreements and disagreements with others can be distinguished and identified. Second, I want also to show that such a theory of justice has in fact actually been held, that it is not an invention of mine, but actually occurs in the literature on justice.

To accomplish these aims, I will construct a paradigm or model of each of the basic theories. The result is a dialectical construction and, as such, not the exposition of any particular theory occurring in the literature. It is a limit to which many individual theories approximate, but which in itself is not identical with any one of them. No author writing on justice has ever formulated the fundamental issues in precisely the terms in which they have been stated in Chapter 2. No author answers all of them in those terms. The choice of terms is mine and they are intended to be dialectically neutral and not prejudicial to any theory of justice. So, too, the construction of each of the basic theories is in my words and not those of any one author.

The theory, in each case, however, consists of positions that men have actually advocated in their discussions of justice. Although as I have constructed it, the theory may not appear in the literature, it states propositions that are asserted by many individual theories. It is also true that some authors come closer than others to asserting all the identifying propositions of the basic theory as I have expressed them. Since they realize the paradigm more perfectly than others, I call them the paradigm authors of the theory.

In constructing each of the basic theories, in analyzing and expounding its content, I rely most heavily on the paradigm authors. Not only is the construction of the position based primarily upon their work but the documentation provided as evidence that this position has actually been taken in the literature comes mostly from their writings. In effect, my aim is to show how their work can be read to reveal their adherence to the position that I have identified and constructed.

To repeat, my three basic theories of justice are dialectical constructions, which provide models for distinguishing and identifying the various particular theories of justice. The fact that some of the authors taken as paradigmatic of one of these positions may belong to a more or less definite philosophical school means only that these individual philosophers have come closer than other writers to realizing the model in all its essential respects. It does not mean that other members of the same school will also assume the same position regarding justice, nor that writers of different philosophical persuasions may not also adopt the same basic position regarding justice.

The identification, exposition, and analysis of what I claim are the basic positions on the meaning of justice should be judged primarily by the analysis that is offered of the paradigm authors. I also attempt to classify the theories of other authors. But, in many cases, I do no more than tabulate the theory by the author's name in the appropriate table without attempting to provide the necessary documentation. For the dialectically difficult authors, that is, those who resist classification, I note only that they are difficult to identify positively and unequivocally with only one of the three basic theories. The main weight of my argument is borne by the authors I have taken as paradigmatic.

The documentation of my paradigm authors thus has to fulfill a twofold purpose, and should be judged accordingly. First, it has to show the theories that are truly paradigmatic for the controversy as a whole, that is, support the claim that there are in fact three basic positions about the nature of justice. Second, the authors taken as paradigm for a given position must be shown clearly to advocate that position.

An example will help to make clear this double role. I claim that in the literature one of the few basic positions is that which asserts that legality constitutes the singly most important meaning of justice. In the exposition of this position, as will be seen, I use Hobbes as the paradigm case for documenting the theory. Thus, in effect, I am advancing a double claim: First, that the position Hobbes takes on justice is one of the basic positions to which, in fact, many writers adhere, and, second, that Hobbes provides a clear, forthright, or paradigmatic version of the theory.

One feature in this description is apt to mislead. I do not mean to assert that the Hobbesian theory constitutes one of the basic positions on justice. His theory of justice contains special features, peculiar to him, such as the social contract theory of the state. What I am claiming is rather that in his theory of justice he takes a position that is shared by many in its essentials, although it may differ in details and accidentals. Thus, Alf Ross, for example, agrees with Hobbes in identifying justice with legality, yet differs from him in denying the social contract. Also, and this is the second point, I would claim that Hobbes gives a clearer, fuller, more paradigm version of this position than Ross does. This is not to say that Hobbes's theory is truer or more valid than Ross's, but only that Hobbes comes closer to striking all the identifying notes of the Positive Law position.

The fundamental issues serve to reveal the basic differences regarding the nature of justice. By means of them we can define the basic positions regarding justice. But, needless to say, they are not the only source of difference and disagreement. As has just been indicated, adherents of one and the same theory do not agree at all points. Furthermore, a position on such a disputed point may be shared in common by adherents of otherwise different theories. For example, a Positive Law writer may join with a Social Good author on a given point and oppose other proponents of each of these theories. Thus, besides the fundamental issues that determine the basic positions, there are also certain subsidiary issues on which writers divide into different groups.

In my exposition of the three basic positions, I take note of the more important of these special or subsidiary issues. Main consideration, however, is given to the position taken on the fundamental issues. The others are subsidiary, and kept to a minimum to avoid obscuring the formulation of the basic positions.

In constructing and documenting these positions, I will begin with the Positive Law theory, which in some ways is the least complex; turn next to the Social Good position; and deal last with the Natural Right theory, which is the most complex. In analyzing any one of the theories, some mention is unavoidable of how the theory in question differs from the other two, but such comparison is minimal in the first exposition of the theory. My concern in each case is to establish and understand the particular positions of one basic theory. Confrontation of the three theories with each other and consideration of the three-sided controversy concerning justice is left for the final chapter.

4

The Positive Law Theory
of Justice

THE position of the Positive Law theory regarding the nature of justice is most briefly characterized by the following six propositions:

(1) Justice and injustice are dependent on positive law.
(2) Law itself is independent of justice.
(3) Justice consists in conformity to positive law.
(4) Justice, apart from legality, is merely a subjective norm.
(5) Justice is obligatory ultimately only because of legal and political sanctions.
(6) The virtue of justice is identical with obedience.

The six propositions correspond to the six fundamental issues that we have found to be crucial to the controversy concerning justice. Each one expresses a definite position regarding that issue. The first three make positive law the privileged term for the analysis of justice, the third by implication denying that any other notion is necessary, such as common good or natural right. The fourth and fifth propositions introduce further complications, to account for senses of justice

other than that of conformity to the positive law. The sixth characterizes justice as a virtue.

The Positive Law theory of justice thus consists fundamentally of
two parts: one, an account of justice in terms of positive law, and, two,
a theory of meaning that explains other normative uses of the term as
indeterminate and subjective. The second part is essential to the theory as a whole, although it introduces a complicating factor and shows
that the theory is by no means as simple as the name, or the first part,
would indicate.

The six propositions provide the minimal statement of the position,
i.e., the least that is necessary to constitute the Positive Law theory.
To count as an adherent of the theory, one would have to be willing to
assert all six propositions. Yet, as a matter of fact, in the whole
literature on justice there is not a single author who asserts explicitly
all six propositions. Hobbes comes closest to stating all of them. Yet, as
far as I have been able to discover, even he does not explicitly consider
the question of what people mean when they attribute justice or
injustice to laws, and, accordingly, he does not develop the theory
lying behind the fourth proposition as explicitly and fully as others.

How, then, can it be claimed that the fourth proposition is essential
to the Positive Law theory of justice and that Hobbes is one of the
clearest and most forceful adherents of the theory? It can be done, of
course, only by maintaining that if Hobbes had bothered to consider
the question, he would have answered it as in the fourth proposition.
Not only is there nothing in his theory of justice that would deny it
but all that he has to say on the other issues of justice, summed up in
the other propositions, is in accord with it. An even stronger claim can
be made, namely, that the theory of justice that Hobbes puts forward
demands the fourth proposition for its completion. It is not sufficient
merely to identify justice with legality. One must also account for the
fact that justice is used in other senses. Other writers, coming after
Hobbes, such as Kelsen and Alf Ross, have clearly seen this need and
endeavored to meet it.

Writers on justice rarely cover exactly the same range of topics.
Each has his own preferred set of questions. For the Positive Law
theorists, as is to be expected, this set is largely concerned with law.
Yet there are writers, of whom Kelsen and Alf Ross are leading
examples, who clearly take the Positive Law position on the issues of
justice involving law and yet are also concerned to argue that justice
in any other sense must be only a subjective expression of attitude. In

other words, they devote considerable attention to the elaboration of the fourth proposition.

Later writers are more complete than Hobbes only in this one respect. Usually, in their own exposition, they fail to treat one of the fundamental issues on which Hobbes does explicitly take a position, such as the sixth issue regarding justice as a virtue.

All this is only by way of noting and emphasizing that the position determined by the six propositions is a dialectical construction, representing a pure or ideal position, toward which many writers on justice approach, but which no one actually states in so many words. Although individual writers have their own special terminology and their own preferred questions, it is possible to ascertain from what they do say the position they would take on the other issues on which they are silent. An author rarely neglects more than one or two of the fundamental issues, and what he has to say on the other four or five suffices to indicate his position on the others.

With the qualifications just indicated, the following writers can be classified as holding the Positive Law theory of justice; that is, their own theories tend toward the position characterized by the six identifying propositions given above, even though they may not assert them explicitly:

PROPONENTS OF THE POSITIVE LAW THEORY

Amos	Holmes
Austin	Ihering**
Ayer	Kelsen
Bobbio	Markaby
Clark	Paton
Glaucon*	Robertson
Gray	Roguin
Hearn	Alf Ross
Hegel**	Salmond
Hobbes	Spinoza
Hohfeld	Thrasymachus*
Holland	

* Not an author, of course, but of such importance to the dialectical construction of the theory that he is eminently worth including, even though only a speaker in a Platonic dialogue.

** One of the dialectically difficult authors, and, hence, especially subject to the qualifications of classification noted in Chapter 2, p. 22.

In the exposition and elucidation of the theory, we have two main aims: First, to present the Positive Law theory of justice in such a way that it can be seen and judged, not only for itself and on its own but also in relation to the other basic positions regarding justice; and, second, to show that such a theory has actually been held, that is, to provide documentary evidence for the existence of such a position in the literature on justice.

For documentation I appeal almost entirely to those authors who come closest to actually asserting all six of the fundamental propositions. They represent what I have called the paradigm authors of the Positive Law theory of justice. Of these, Hobbes is the most important, and, after him, Austin and Kelsen.

The heart of the theory lies in the claim that positive law can explain all the important uses of the term "justice." The attempt to substantiate this claim can be viewed as having three moments: First, the claim that justice depends upon law and is posterior to it; second, that law itself, being prior to justice, cannot be judged in terms of justice; and, third, that law provides the whole measure of justice so that it consists in nothing but conformity to law.

The three points are closely related, so closely that what an author writes in support of one is almost certain to contain material bearing on the other two. As will be seen when we come to document the positions, one and the same text can often be cited in support of any one of them, and that it appears in one place rather than another is more a matter of emphasis than anything else. Yet the three points are distinct. The first consists in the claim that questions of justice, in any important sense, only arise in connection with law, and, if all laws were taken away, justice would cease to exist. The second point is the independence of law itself from justice—law, it is maintained, not being itself just or unjust. Since justice is said to be found only where there is law, and law itself is not subject to justice, it is then claimed, as the third moment, that law provides the whole norm of justice so that to decide whether or not an action is just one need only determine whether or not it conforms to the law. Justice then is accurately and adequately defined as conformity to law.

The construction of the Positive Law theory of justice calls first, then, for the analysis of these three moments. We want to see how the theory defends its threefold claim; or, in other words, how it proposes to establish its position on the first three fundamental issues concerning justice.

The Dependence of Justice on Law

Hobbes defends the proposition that justice depends on law by seeking to describe what conditions would be like in a situation where no law existed. In such a situation there would be "no common power," no organized society capable of issuing commands and enforcing them, and men would live in what he calls "the state of nature." Lacking any overriding social rules, men would oppose each other only as individuals, and, according to Hobbes, men as individuals seek their own advantage; they are avid for gain, safety, and reputation. But men, individually, are so equal in power that no one enjoys a clear advantage; also, no one is safe or secure; the life of all is "solitary, poor, nasty, brutish, and short:"[1] Hence, the state of nature amounts to a state of war, and "such a war as is of every man against every man."[2]

In the state of nature there is no common power able to make laws and enforce them. There is also no justice or injustice. "Before the names of just and unjust can have place," Hobbes writes, "there must be some coercive power to compel men equally to the performance of their covenants." As long as "there is a fear of not performance on either part," there can be no question of justice: "Injustice actually there can be none till the cause of such fear be taken away."[3] In war, and the state of nature is a state of war, "force and fraud are . . . the two cardinal virtues." Since a man may then do anything he can to preserve his own life, "nothing can be unjust," Hobbes asserts.[4]

The dependence of justice upon the existence of a superior power is supported by this counterfactual argument: "If we could suppose a great multitude of men to consent in the observation of justice . . . without a common power to keep them all in awe, we might as well suppose all mankind to do the same; and then there neither would be nor need to be any civil government or commonwealth at all."[5] Hobbes obviously intends the impossibility of the consequent to prove the absurdity of the antecedent. Men only too obviously need government to order their relations with one another.

The remedy for the "ill condition which man by mere nature is

1 *Leviathan*, pp. 94, 97.
2 *Ibid.*, p. 66.
3 *Ibid.*, p. 110.
4 *Ibid.*, p. 38.
5 *Ibid.*, pp. 129–130.

actually placed in" is plain from the disease. What is wanting is a common power. This is obtained through the establishment of a "commonwealth," or what we would usually now call a civil society or state, and which Hobbes also calls "Leviathan," to emphasize its power. This Leviathan comes into being by the social contract, or the common agreement of men to abandon the state of nature. According to Hobbes, this is "a covenant of every man with every man in such manner as if every man should say to every man, 'I authorize and give up my right of governing myself to this man, or to this assembly of men, on this condition that you give up your right to him and authorize all his actions in like manner.' " Thus Leviathan is born and "has the use of so much power and strength conferred on him that by terror thereof, he is enabled to form the wills of them all, the peace at home and mutual aid against their enemies abroad."⁶ There is "coercive power to compel men equally to the performance of their covenants" and hence occasion for justice.⁷

Without a power of enforcement, there is, according to Hobbes, no ground for covenant or private contract between individuals. "Covenants, being but words and breath, have no force to oblige, contain, constrain, or protect any man, but what it has from the public sword,"⁸ and without this they are vain and invalid.

Such a claim asserts a position on the source of obligation, which is an issue that we have reserved for later consideration. But it also supplies a reason for the dependence of justice upon power, and with it still another argument for the dependence of justice upon law. Without a superior coercive power, there is not only no ground for private contract, there is also no ground, strictly speaking, for property. In the state of "mere nature," according to Hobbes, "every man has right to everything." But this is tantamount to having no right at all, if right is understood as establishing a claim for performance upon some other basis than the strength to enforce it. Hence there is no basis on which a man can claim anything as his own by right. There is no *mine* and *thine*, no property, since by property we mean, Hobbes says, "the rules whereby every man may know what goods he may enjoy and what actions he may do without being molested by any of his fellow subjects."⁹

⁶ *Ibid.*, p. 132.
⁷ *Ibid.*, pp. 110–111.
⁸ *Ibid.*, p. 135.
⁹ *Ibid.*, p. 137.

This much may be gathered, Hobbes contends, from "the ordinary definition of justice," by which he refers to that of Ulpian, which is preserved in the Roman Law. Justice is there defined as the constant will of giving to every man his own. Hobbes continues that "where there is no own, that is, no property, there is no injustice; and where there is no coercive power erected, that is, where there is no commonwealth, there is no property, all men having right to all things. Therefore, where there is no commonwealth, there is nothing unjust."[10]

Hobbes thus would be willing to accept the Roman definition of justice provided it is understood that it is law that determines what is one's own, and not vice versa. "Rules of property," Hobbes writes, "or *meum* and *tuum*, and of good, evil, lawful, and unlawful in the actions of subjects are the civil laws, that is to say, the laws of each commonwealth in particular."[11]

If we think of men existing in a condition where they are utterly without law, then, according to the Positive Law theory, we will see that there can be no question of justice or injustice. In other words, justice and injustice depend upon law, and hence are the work of civil society and relative to it. Without society, *i.e.,* in a state of nature, there is no justice. Given different societies, there are different "justices." There are too many different ideas of justice, Kelsen claims, for one to be able to speak simply of justice. The "basic norm" of a society determines what is just and unjust: "A man is just if his behavior conforms to the norms of a social order supposed to be just."[12] But every society believes that its order is just. Justice then is relative to a given society and to the kind of constitution it has. A democratic society has "democratic justice"; an oligarchic society, "oligarchic justice"; a communist society, "communist justice."

The Independence of Law from Justice

Law itself, according to the Positive Law theory, is independent of justice. Justice is not a criterion of law that measures it and determines whether it is just or unjust. It is not a source or ideal that positive law endeavors to declare and realize in practice. In fact, for

10 *Ibid.,* pp. 110–111.
11 *Ibid.,* p. 137.
12 *What is Justice?,* p. 2.

the adherents of the Positive Law theory, there is something wrong, mistaken, even paradoxical, and nonsensical, about calling law itself just or unjust.

"No law can be unjust," Hobbes declares.[13] This proposition, John Austin comments, "has been deemed by many an immoral or pernicious paradox"; yet if we consider it carefully, he claims, we must admit that it is "neither pernicious nor paradoxical, but is merely a truism put in unguarded terms." It means that "no *positive* law is *legally* unjust," and this is "indisputably true," Austin declares, "for positive law is the measure or test of legal justice and injustice: and, consequently, if positive law might be legally unjust, positive law might be unjust as measured or tried by itself."[14]

Kelsen makes the same point, in declaring that " 'justice' means legality."[15] This being so, to ask whether a law is unjust amounts to asking whether the particular law is a law. That a law is a law is an empty tautology for Kelsen. "The question whether a given law is just or not," he writes, "cannot be answered scientifically at all."[16]

The fact that Kelsen says the question cannot be answered "scientifically" is important for understanding the Positive Law theory of justice. Austin allows that the flat assertion that no law is unjust is expressed in unguarded terms, and the Positive Law theory is misunderstood if it is taken to deny that laws are ever *called* just or unjust. It is a fact that people do make such judgments, and the Positive Law theory can admit this and also offer an explanation of what they mean. Thus, Austin, for example, admits that "the same act may be just and unjust as tried by different measures." It "may be just as agreeing with a given law, although the act itself, and the law with which it agrees, are both of them unjust as compared with a different rule."[17] Austin cites the case of a law and its corresponding act being judged by the rules of morality or by divine law.

Although the Positive Law theory can allow that law may be subjected to another standard of justice, it claims that any standard other than the positive law is neither determinate nor objective; it is not "scientific," as Kelsen says. What makes this theory unique and distinct from all other theories of justice is precisely the claim that

13 *Op. cit.*, p. 268.
14 *The Province of Jurisprudence Determined,* pp. 260–261, note.
15 *General Theory of Law and State,* p. 14.
16 *Ibid.,* p. 6.
17 *Op. cit.,* pp. 262–263, note.

positive law suffices by itself, independently of any other measure, to establish the only determinate and objective norm of justice. In Hobbes's words, "the laws are the rules of just and unjust."[18] Any other meaning of justice is, on this theory, indeterminate and subjective, as we shall see when we come to consider the fourth fundamental issue.

Law, then, is independent of justice, and it is a mistake, according to the Positive Law theory, to hold that the pursuit of justice constitutes the purpose of law. Law, of course, has a purpose, and how well it furthers that purpose may well provide a basis for judging the goodness of the law. But, as Hobbes remarks explicitly, the goodness of a law is not the same as its justice.[19]

How can the Positive Law theory of justice maintain that the goodness of a law is not the same as its justice? If the reason were merely verbal—the Positive Law writers disliking the word "justice" when talking of the purpose of law—the relation between justice and law would cease to constitute a fundamental issue dividing the Positive Law theory from other major theories of justice. We need to show that the purpose of law, for the Positive Law theory, does not provide a criterion external to the law by which it can be measured and, to the extent that it reaches or falls short, judged to be just or unjust. More must be involved, for our purposes, than mere dislike for the word. In short, why can Hobbes maintain that a bad law is not an unjust law?

For Hobbes, the purpose of law is identical with that of the fundamental compact underlying the founding of the state, namely, the pursuit and establishment of peace and order. But, apart from law, that is, in the state of nature, there is no peace, but only war and disorder. Peace in that condition is at most an indeterminate ideal, a wish of those engaged in the ceaseless battle. It is law, and law alone, that produces peace and order. Peace is not something external and separate from law by which it can be measured, but the very fruition of law itself. A bad law, then, is only one that has failed to produce the peace and order that are needed. If, as Kelsen claims, "there is a definite tendency to identify . . . the ideal of peace for that of justice,"[20] it might even be said that a bad law is one that does not

[18] *Op. cit.,* p. 204.
[19] See *op. cit.,* p. 268.
[20] *Op. cit.,* p. 14.

make all the justice that is needed. But the important point, here, is that it is the law itself that makes justice, and, until a regime of law exists, there is no justice at all by which to measure anything else, let alone the law. Thus, as we have seen, it is characteristic of the Positive Law theory to claim that measuring the law by justice amounts to measuring the law by itself.

Not all adherents of the theory agree about the primary purpose of law. For Hobbes, it is peace and security; for Austin, the general utility, and, for Kelsen, social happiness. But all agree that apart from law such a purpose is indeterminate, ineffective, and subjective, even empty. It takes law to provide a substantive meaning and establish a criterion clear and definite enough to serve as a measure of human action, such as is demanded of the norm of justice.

The Positive Law theory requires that justice be objective and determinate so as to provide a precise criterion for determining whether an action is just or unjust. Only the law itself, they claim, meets this requirement. In comparison with the law, any other criterion, including their own specification of the purpose of law, is indeterminate and subjective. Law alone provides the norm of justice for the Positive Law theory because only the positive law is determinate and objective. One could be an adherent of the theory and deny that there is any other norm at all. But this extreme position is not essential or necessary to the theory. All that is required is the assertion that positive law is not only the most important term for analyzing the meaning of justice but it also establishes the norm of justice itself.

It is also worth noting that, in denying that justice provides a criterion of law, the theory also holds, as a consequence, that justice cannot properly be said to be a standard or ideal for the legislator. With regard to law itself, justice can provide a standard only for its execution and application, not for its making as such. "Justice in the sense of legality," Kelsen writes, "is a quality which relates not to the content of a positive order, but to its application. . . . [and] means the maintenance of a positive order by conscientious application of it."[21]

When the question arises whether a law has been properly applied, whether it has been violated or not, one appeals for decision to a judge sitting in a "court of justice." According to the Positive Law theory, justice does provide a criterion of the judge's activity. Alf Ross writes:

[21] *Ibid.*

"The words 'just' and 'unjust' . . . make sense when applied to characterize the decision that is made by a judge—or any other persons dealing with the application of a given set of rules. To say that the decision is just means that it has been made in regular fashion, that is, in conformity with the rule or system of rules in force." It is an entirely different matter, however, when they are applied to a legislator or to his work: "Applied to characterize a general rule or order, the words 'just' or 'unjust' are entirely devoid of meaning. Justice is no guide for the legislator. . . . Applied in this connection (*i.e.*, with regard to the content of the rule or order), the words have no descriptive meaning at all."[22]

It might appear odd to hold that a judge can be just or unjust, while a legislator can only be good or bad and never just or unjust. Yet the Positive Law theory is not inconsistent in making this claim. Justice implies conformity to a rule, and, for the Positive Law theory, the law provides a rule for the judge, but not for the legislator who makes the rule: the judge is under the law, the legislator above it, at least when making it.

The Positive Law theory accordingly tends to restrict many traditional principles of justice to the work of the judge. This is especially true of the principle of equality.

Hobbes writes that "it cannot be denied but that justice is a certain equality," but then limits it drastically to the claim "that since we are all equal by nature, one should not arrogate more right to himself than he grants to another, unless he have fairly gotten it by compact."[23] He expressly denies that equality by itself, apart from legal enactment, is a norm for economic practice: "As if it were injustice to sell dearer than we buy, or to give more to a man than he merits. The value of all things contracted for is measured by the appetite of the contractors, and therefore the just value is that which they be contented to give."[24] Yet Hobbes does find that equality is demanded of the judge or arbitrator, whose work he identifies as that of distributive justice. The judge should establish "equity" which issues in "just distribution." Equity is included among Hobbes's nineteen laws of nature. Of it, he writes: "If a man be trusted to judge between man and man, it is a precept of the law of nature that he deal equally

22 *On Law and Justice*, p. 274.
23 *De cive*, Ch. 3, No. 6.
24 *Leviathan*, p. 115.

between them."[25] He enumerates still further qualities of a good judge, such as contempt of wealth and position, disinterestedness, patience, etc. In all these demands, Hobbes seems to be requiring that a judge interpret and apply the law equally and impartially.[26]

Kelsen claims that "equality before the law or lawfulness is nothing but the logical law of contradiction with reference to the application of a general norm of positive law to particular cases." Suppose, he argues, that the law demands that every individual more than fourteen years old who commits theft should be punished. If, now, C and D, both being more than fourteen years old, should commit theft, "then the judgment is true that not only C but also D shall be punished." From this, Kelsen concludes that "the judgment that it is not just to decide that C shall be punished, but D shall not be punished, only means: "It is contradictory."[27] The requirement of equality in the application of law thus is reduced to a purely formal requirement. For equality to mean any more than this, Kelsen claims, positive law is necessary to spell out the particular respects in which equality is to be observed and sought.

Justice, on the Positive Law theory, is not a criterion of the law, nor of the legislator. Hence, it is also no criterion of the state as such. States cannot be just or unjust, any more than laws can, for the state is the lawmaking power and, hence, is itself the source of justice.

Thus, Hobbes claims that "nothing the sovereign representative can do to a subject, on what pretense soever, can properly be called injustice or injury, because every subject is author of every act the sovereign does."[28] But the "sovereign representative" is identical with the sovereign or state itself, and Hobbes can accordingly be understood as saying that the state cannot be called unjust.

Kelsen, for example, asks how an order to pay taxes differs from the threat of a gangster or the request of a friend. The only difference, he claims, lies in "the juristic concept of law as it is, in fact, present in the minds of the individuals involved. Sociologically, the decisive difference between the three cases is the fact that the behavior of the taxpayer is determined—or at least accompanied—by the idea of a valid order, of norm, duty, authority, whereas his behavior in the

---

[25] *Ibid.*, p. 119.
[26] See *ibid.*, p. 217.
[27] *What is Justice?*, pp. 133–134; cf. *General Theory of Law and State*, p. 439.
[28] *Op. cit.*, p. 163.

other cases is not determined or accompanied by such an idea."[29] It is the belief in the taxpayer's mind that the order issues from a valid lawmaking authority which makes the difference.

According to Alf Ross, there is no objective answer to the question whether a given state is a legal order or a regime of violence. It "depends on the way it is experienced by the individual, and the same order can be both to different individuals."[30]

On the Positive Law theory, it does not make sense, objectively, to speak of the state as just or unjust. Yet this claim does not mean that an adherent of the theory holds that all states and forms of government are equally preferable, and that there is nothing to choose from between them. Kelsen gives vigorous support to "the justice of freedom, the justice of peace, the justice of democracy, the justice of tolerance,"[31] but he maintains that this conviction, however strongly it may be held, is only his subjective personal preference, and has no objective basis in fact, since it involves a value judgment, which, as such, is completely removed from the realm of fact.

CONFORMITY TO LAW

We have seen that the Positive Law theory holds that questions of justice arise only in connection with law, and that law itself is independent of justice. We come now to the third moment and the position that law provides the whole measure of justice; in other words, that justice consists in conformity to law. To see that this, in fact, is maintained by the theory is readily done, since all that has gone before provides a preparation for precisely this claim.

Hobbes declares explicitly that "nothing is reputed unjust that is not contrary to some law,"[32] so that "just" said of a man means "he that in his actions observes the laws of his country."[33] He equates injustice with crime which he identifies as "the committing, by deed or word, of that which the law forbids, or the omission of what it has commanded."[34]

[29] *General Theory of Law and State*, p. 176.
[30] *Op. cit.*, p. 56.
[31] *What is Justice?*, p. 24.
[32] *Op. cit.*, p. 204.
[33] *Ibid.*, p. 26.
[34] *Ibid.*, p. 224.

"Law is itself the standard of justice," Austin writes.[35] "Whenever it is uttered with a determinate meaning, it is uttered with relation to a determinate law which the speaker assumes as a standard of comparison."[36]

On this point, Kelsen also agrees with Hobbes and Austin. He claims that justice "means legality," when it is withdrawn from "the insecure realm of subjective judgments of value" and established "on the secure ground of a given social order."[37] In fact, he asserts that his theory "eliminates the dualism of law and justice."[38]

There is also no question that the only law at issue is the positive law. According to Hobbes, the civil law provides "the rules of just and unjust," and, for him, the civil law "is to every subject those rules which the commonwealth has commanded him, by word, writing, or other sufficient sign of the will, to make use of for the distinction of right and wrong; that is to say, of what is contrary and what is not contrary to rule."[39] Austin does speak, in fact, of both divine and natural law, as well as of positive law, but he maintains that natural law is too indeterminate to provide a determinate sense of justice, whereas, if divine law is determinate for him, it is because it is also positively instituted; law "strictly and simply and exclusively," such as provides a determinate standard of justice, "applies to rules set by a political superior," which comprise what Austin calls the positive law.[40] For Kelsen, as we shall see, there is no law but positive law.

In identifying justice with conformity to the law, the Positive Law theory expressly denies the adequacy of the ancient and common definition of justice as rendering to each his own—*suum cuique*. Hobbes, as we have seen, claims that this definition already presupposes law, since it is only through law that anyone has anything he can claim as his *own*: Property, he writes, consists in "the constitution of *mine* and *thine* and *his*," and is "an effect of commonwealth, which can do nothing but by the person that represents it . . . and consists in the laws, which none can make that have not the sovereign power."[41]

---

[35] *The Province of Jurisprudence Determined,* p. 190.
[36] *Ibid.,* pp. 261–262, *infra.*
[37] *Op. cit.,* p. 14.
[38] *Ibid.,* p. xvi.
[39] *Op. cit.,* pp. 203–204.
[40] See *op. cit.,* pp. 11–12.
[41] *Op. cit.,* pp. 189–190.

But if the *suum* derives its meaning only from law, in itself and apart from law it must be empty, at least as part of a formula offered as a definition of justice. Thus, Kelsen refers to *suum cuique* as an "empty formula," since it "does not answer the question as to what is everybody's own." Kelsen goes on to say that "almost all the famous formulas defining justice presuppose the expected answer as self-evident. But the answer is not at all self-evident. In fact, the answer to the question as to what is everybody's own, as to what is to be the content of the general principles binding on all men, as to what is right and what is wrong—the answer to all these questions is supposed to be given by positive law."[42] He asserts even more strongly that "without presupposing the existence of a positive legal order, all these formulas are devoid of sense."[43]

To deny that *suum* has any content apart from law, that is, that any person can claim anything as his own independent of its incorporation within a legal system, is in effect to deny that there is such a thing as natural right. At the very least, to claim possession of a natural right is to hold that one has a right to something in virtue of being a man or a person, independently or distinct from being a citizen of a state and subject to its laws. To claim a natural right is to assert a right that is not the creation of the positive law. It is to claim possession of something as one's own, so to speak, on one's own. It is for this reason that the Roman or Ulpian definition of justice is defended by the Natural Right theory of justice as peculiarly its own. Hence, the position that the Positive Law theory adopts with regard to the *suum cuique* definition constitutes a denial of natural right.

The point is obviously of major importance for our dialectical and taxonomic endeavor, since it is this very denial that provides the mark for distinguishing the Positive Law theory from the Natural Right theory of justice. It is, therefore, important to see that the paradigm authors of the theory do in fact make such a denial. This is readily accomplished in the case of Kelsen, since his denial of natural right is loud and insistent. But it is much less easy when we come to Hobbes and Austin, since both in so many words seem to assert the existence of natural right. Yet, as I hope to show, there is good ground in their writings for claiming that they do deny natural right as a basis of justice.

[42] *Op. cit.*, p. 10.
[43] *Ibid.*, p. 416.

We begin with Kelsen, since his denial of natural right is explicit. "The rights and duties of man, established by . . . natural law," he writes, "are considered to be innate or inborn in man, because implanted by nature and not imposed or conferred upon him by a human legislator; and insofar as nature manifests God's will, these rights and duties are sacred."[44] These rights and duties, or rather their observance, are supposed to constitute an ideal "just order." But the difficulty, according to Kelsen, is that "none of the numerous natural law theories has so far succeeded in defining the content of this just order" in an objective and determinate way.[45] In fact, he denies that any "rational justification" of it is possible, since it is founded on "self deception, or what amounts to the same thing, it is an ideology."[46] What is presented as an ideally just order is "only the expression of certain group or class interests" which rest at bottom on "judgments of value which have no objectivity."[47] In other words, the Natural Law theory of natural rights cannot provide an objective system of norms, a normative order, such as the positive law provides.[48] Any determination of justice as involving conformity to an objective norm must, accordingly, consist in conformity to the positive law.

Kelsen clearly wants nothing to do with the notion of natural right or natural law. Austin, however, does admit the term "natural law," although I have found no actual use of the term "natural right." Yet, although he might use them, he would deny that either one provides a basis for justice, at least in a clear, determinate, and objective sense. He speaks of the "fancied *jus naturale*" occurring at the beginning of the second of Justinian's *Institutes,* where Ulpian's celebrated definition of justice also occurs, and notes that it is "a name for the instincts of animals." Allowing that instincts are sometimes called laws, he claims that they are so only "by slender or remote analogy" and should not be confounded with "laws properly so called."[49] He also notes that there are "legal and moral rules which are nearly or quite universal and the expediency of which must be seen by merely natural reason, or by reason without the lights of extensive experience and observation." Austin allows that this fact provides some ground for

[44] *Ibid.,* p. 9.
[45] *Ibid.*
[46] *Ibid.,* p. 8.
[47] *Ibid.,* p. 11.
[48] *Ibid.,* p. xiv.
[49] *Op. cit.,* pp. 176–177.

drawing a distinction between natural and positive law. But since this fact is explained as "the offspring of a moral instinct or sense, or of innate practical principles," which he believes is false, he demands the expulsion from the sciences of jurisprudence and morality of the very term "natural law" as "misleading and pernicious jargon."[50]

Austin also admits that divine law and the principles of morality may be used as measures by which to test the justice of a law. It might appear then that he would have to admit that there is a basis for natural right, apart from positive law. Yet, according to him, the basis is unsound, and he dismisses it for the same reason that he refuses to approve the term "natural law." It fails to meet the standard of clearness, determinateness, and objectivity that he demands for the norm of justice: "Moral obligation is anything which we choose to call so, for the precepts of positive morality are infinitely varying, and the will of God, whether indicated by utility or by a moral sense, is equally matter of dispute."[51]

Hobbes's doctrine of natural right and natural law is much more difficult to understand. In fact, the interpretation of it, as well as his motive for appropriating at least the language of the traditional teaching on the subject, has long provided a famous crux in Hobbesian scholarship. But his use of natural law and natural right can be so interpreted as to be consistent with his position on the previous issues and, at the same time, as fundamentally opposed to the Natural Right theory concerning the basis of justice.

Hobbes introduces his discussion of natural laws *à propos* of considering the causes that would lead men to abandon the solitary "state of nature" with its war of all against all. They are then "laws" that apply to man prior to his living together with other men in civil society. These "laws" that lead men to enter a life of society he describes as "the passions that incline men to peace," such as the fear of death, desire of commodious living, and the hope of winning this by their own industry, together with certain "suggestions" of reason that provide "convenient articles of peace upon which men may be drawn to agreement."[52] Here, he speaks of the laws of nature as "passions" and "suggestions of reason." Elsewhere, he also notes that they "are not properly laws, but qualities that dispose men to peace and to

---

[50] *Ibid.*, pp. 178–179.
[51] *Ibid.*, pp. 190–191.
[52] *Op. cit.*, p. 98.

obedience"[53]—or "conclusions or theorems concerning what conduceth to the conservation and defence of themselves."[54] From this it appears that Hobbes's laws of nature consist of what Austin refers to as natural instincts and general principles of expediency. Further, it is clear that the nineteen laws Hobbes enumerates and comments upon are not all equally "natural," either in the sense of being innate or independent of civil society. The fourteenth law, for example, is the provision for primogeniture, while the nineteenth concerns the proper number of witnesses a judge should hear for the determination of fact. Hobbes himself does not give equal weight to all of them, and, in fact, contends that all of them can be summarized in the injunction: "Do not that to another which you would not have done to yourself"[55]—*i.e.*, the Golden Rule.

The "fountain and original of justice" is identified with the third law of nature. The first inclines men "to endeavor peace"; the second, "to transfer to another such rights, as being retained, hinder the peace of mankind." From this, Hobbes claims, the third follows, "that men perform their covenants made." This provides the basis of justice, he argues, because until there is the fundamental covenant establishing civil society, no transfer of right has occurred and "every man has a right to everything," which is tantamount to no right at all, if this is taken as making a claim upon other persons on some basis besides that of physical force. Consequently, Hobbes declares, "no action can be unjust. But when a covenant is made, then to break it is unjust. And the definition of injustice is no other than the not performance of covenant."[56] How, it may be asked, does this definition square with Hobbes's previous definition of justice (p. 55, *supra*) as observance of law? To show that they are equivalent will also show that positive law constitutes the basis of justice.

Hobbes explains the fundamental covenant as a transfer of right: man lays down his "right to all things" and is "contented with so much liberty against other men as he would allow other men against himself."[57] The right in question is a "natural" right in that it belongs to men in a state of nature. Hobbes uses the term in still different senses, none of which is the same as understood in the Natural Right

53 *Ibid.*, p. 205.
54 *Ibid.*, pp. 122–123.
55 *Ibid.*, pp. 121, 208–209.
56 *Ibid.*, p. 110.
57 *Ibid.*, p. 100.

theory. It is sometimes equivalent to a power or ability as consisting in the liberty to act or forbear without external impediment.[58] When it is compared to law as liberty to obligation, right is taken as the complete absence of obligation. Yet, in being given up to the sovereign, right is also supposed to create an obligation.[59] In accord with the first law of nature, this right consists in "the liberty which each man has to use his own power, as he will himself, for the preservation of his own . . . life," including, if need be, the "right to everything, even to one another's body."[60] By giving up and abandoning the exercise of this right, men, according to Hobbes, enter into a compact with one another that establishes civil society as a power to make laws and bind them to their observance. Hence for them to keep their covenant consists precisely in observing the commands of the sovereign. There is no difference between keeping the covenant and observing the law except the terms of reference—one being to the subject's bond, the other to the correlative law that he binds himself to perform.

From this it is clear that natural right is not the basis for justice in Hobbes, as understood by the Natural Right theory. For him, the critical term for the analysis of justice is not right but covenant or law—law being "brought into the world for nothing else, but to limit the natural liberty of particular men," and to deprive them of that "right of nature that is the natural liberty of men."[61] If, then, Hobbes claims that natural law or right is the "fountain and original of justice," it is only in the sense of being a prior condition that leads to the establishment of a norm of justice, but this norm itself is provided by law, not by natural right. In talking about the source of justice, he has in mind the condition of men living in a state of nature prior to the establishment of a regime of law, where there is no question of justice or injustice, and of their reasons and motives for departing from such a state. "Law of nature" is here said metaphorically to be "the fountain and original of justice" only in the sense of being the condition in which men lived before they entered into civil society, with its laws establishing rules of justice. Laws of nature, in this sense, provide no measure or criterion of justice, except in the negative sense of being something that men want to escape from.

[58] See *ibid.*, p. 99.
[59] See *ibid.*; cf. pp. 222–223.
[60] *Ibid.*, p. 99.
[61] *Ibid.*, p. 206.

Nature supplies no positive basis for justice as it does in the Natural Right theory.

We shall have to return to Hobbes's conception of natural law when we come to consider the obligatoriness of justice. But we have seen enough to establish that natural right does not provide a positive criterion of justice for Hobbes any more than it does for Austin or Kelsen.

We have now completed our construction of the position of the Positive Law theory on the fundamental issues relating law and justice. Justice on this theory is best and most adequately defined and considered as consisting in conformity to positive law. Since this contention is expressly denied by both the Social Good and the Natural Right theories of justice, this assertion by itself establishes the Positive Law theory as a distinct and different position from either of them. At the same time, we have also seen the heart or center of the position in examining the theory on the relation between justice and law. Yet our task is still only half completed. As noted before, the Positive Law theory contains a negative as well as a positive part. Besides maintaining that law provides the basic meaning of justice, it also denies that there is any other sense or use of justice that establishes an objective norm of human action. To show that law provides the only objective meaning of justice, we have to see, not only that law does set an objective standard but also that no other sense of justice can do so. To the latter part of that task we now turn.

THE SUBJECTIVITY OF JUSTICE

If justice, objectively, means nothing but legality, is there any real need for such terms as "justice" and its cognates? Could not these words be eliminated entirely and their place taken, without loss, by "legality" and its cognates? Why, on the Positive Law theory of justice, should there be any concern at all for the word "justice?"

Adherents of the theory may write at times as though such a drastic elimination not only could but should be undertaken. Yet they also acknowledge, if only implicitly, that something would be lost, and that to say that an action is just implies something more than that it is legal.

That "just" means more than "legal" is plain from the way the words are employed in quite ordinary usage. For one thing, we may admit that a given action is legal without thereby approving of it. It is normal for people to disapprove of those who take advantage of the law to their own profit and to the discomfort, if not actual hurt, of others. We could well say of such an action not only that it is legal but also that it is bad. This fact alone is enough to show that the term "legal" cannot entirely replace the word "just." For to say that an action is just is also to indicate that it is good and that one approves of it. As we have already noted, its approbative character is one of the common notes of justice. Thus, even on the Positive Law theory, which bases justice on law, to say that X is just is to say not only that X is legal but also that it is something good and approved of.

The point that justice is somehow more than legality, even on the Positive Law theory, appears most clearly and explicitly in Kelsen's analysis. He notes that we commonly make value judgments of social behavior and call good "that conduct in accordance with the order" or norm, and bad "that contrary to the order." Hence, he claims, "conformity to the order is usually connected with the approval of one's fellow-men; non-conformity with their disapproval."[62] Furthermore, in announcing that his purpose is to present "the law as it is, without defending it by calling it just, or condemning it by terming it unjust," he thereby admits that the term "just" performs an evaluative function. By using it, we manifest our attitude to the object to which it is applied, show that it is something we judge as good and that we approve of and would defend. This is obviously more than can be said of our use of "legal."

Although not as explicit as Kelsen, both Hobbes and Austin also recognize the evaluative character of justice. According to Hobbes, justice is a good, but "*good* and *evil* are names that signify our appetites and aversions," and we praise something by calling it good or "dispraise and call evil."[63] Austin, as we have seen, holds that justice means primarily conformity to some standard. But he too allows that we use the term "to express our own approbation," and what is even worse, according to him, we may use it only for this purpose and "signify mere dislike, which it would be far better to signify by a grunt or a groan than by a mischievous and detestable abuse of articulate language."[64]

[62] *Op. cit.*, pp. 15–16.
[63] *Op. cit.*, p. 122.
[64] *The Province of Jurisprudence Determined*, p. 190.

The Positive Law theory thus recognizes that there is an approba-tive factor in justice in addition to that of legality. It also claims, as Austin's last text indicates, that it is possible for the two factors to be disjoined and used separately, and this possibility furnishes the Posi-tive Law theory with an explanation of what people mean when they assert that law itself is just or unjust. By this, they can only mean that they approve or disapprove of the law, since, according to the theory, justice consists in legality, and it is senseless to speak of the legality of a law. This much is contained in the passages just cited, but it is asserted even more emphatically by Alf Ross, a disciple of Kelsen, who writes: "A person who maintains that a certain rule or order—for example, a system of taxation—is unjust, does not indicate any discern-ible quality in the order; he does not provide any reasons for his attitude, but merely gives to it an emotional expression. A says: 'I am against this rule because it is unjust.' What he should say is: 'This rule is unjust because I oppose it.' To invoke justice is the same thing as banging on the table: an emotional expression which turns one's demand into an absolute postulate."[65]

Ross, in this passage, makes explicit a further point about approba-tion or approval, which is characteristic of the Positive Law theory: namely, that approbation is entirely subjective and tells nothing at all about the object of which it is expressed, but only about the subject making it.

Any utterance at all reveals something about the utterer. If it is an English expression and the circumstances in which it is uttered show that it is used meaningfully, it reveals that the speaker knows English. Saying "ouch" in suitable circumstances is an indication of pain. But many of our utterances, in addition to revealing something about ourselves, also say something about the world. Saying of a certain person that he is drinking wine tells something about that person. According to Ross and Kelsen, there are also expressions that seem to state something about the world, when, in fact, they do not. They claim that statements of the form, "X is just," are frequently of this kind.

As we have seen, the Positive Law theory allows that the statement "Judge A is just," makes good sense, but it denies that this is true of the statement "Legislator B is just." Both statements do indicate approval of the judge and the legislator; thus they indicate something

[65] *On Law and Justice*, p. 274.

about the speaker. But the similarity between the two expressions goes no further. The one about the judge, it is claimed, tells us something about the judge, whereas that about the legislator does not.

Both statements are normative in intention—the one, in asserting that the judge conforms to the norm for judges, the other, that the legislator conforms to the norm for legislators. But, according to the Positive Law theory, there is a vast difference between the two norms. That for the judge is objective, being identical with legality, *i.e.*, with the basic law of the land. But that for the legislator is purely subjective. In other words, justice has an objective, normative meaning only when it is identical with legality. On any other usage it ceases to have an objective, normative meaning and is subjective only; that is to say, it may reveal something about the speaker, but it says nothing at all about anything else.

Thus, Ross writes: "Applied to characterize a general rule or order, the words 'just' and 'unjust' are entirely devoid of meaning. Justice is no guide for the legislator," and when 'just' and 'unjust' are applied to the legislator or to his legislation, Ross goes on to say, "the words have no descriptive meaning at all"; their only meaning is emotive.[66]

As shown by the distinctions he employs, Ross has adopted a definite theory of meaning. Any extended consideration of it would take us far away from the problem of justice. Even to ask whether the Positive Law theory of justice supposes one particular theory of meaning is beyond our purpose. Kelsen and Ross do definitely hold and advocate what has come to be known as the emotive theory of value, from the name used by A. J. Ayer, in 1935, in *Language, Truth, and Logic*. Whether Hobbes and Austin could be said to agree with it is another question, and it is not one that need concern us. There is really only one point about approbation that bears upon justice, and it is held by Hobbes and Austin, as well as by Kelsen and Ross. It thus provides an identifying or characteristic note of the Positive Law theory.

It consists in the claim that approbation as such is an emotion that is entirely subjective and relative to the individual. Justice in its approbative character thus is entirely subjective. Hence, if the attribution of justice to an object lacks any reference to law, then, according to the Positive Law theory, it cannot be anything more than an expression of subjective emotion. Subjectivity, in the sense of being

[66] *Ibid.*

dependent upon the feeling of the individual, then appears as the predominant note. Austin, as we have seen, thinks that to use "injustice" for anything but legality is to "signify mere dislike, which it would be far better to signify by a grunt or a groan." But a grunt or a groan is obviously nothing but an indication of how an individual feels, and a very indefinite one at that.

Any appeal to justice apart from legality, according to Kelsen, involves a judgment of value, and such a judgment is "determined by emotional factors and is therefore subjective in character, valid only for the judging subject and therefore relative only."[67] The subject may lay claim to objectivity for his judgment by appealing to natural law, but this norm, Kelsen claims, is "a typical illusion, due to an objectivization of subjective interests."[68] Nor does it make any difference if the judgment happens to be shared by many individuals. It is still subjective as relative to the individual, since there is no objective fact backing up the judgment. Such a lack in justice, according to Kelsen, sharply distinguishes it from the positive law, whose "contents can be uniquely ascertained by an objective method. The existence of the values of law is conditioned by objectively verifiable facts. To the norms of positive law there corresponds a certain social reality, but not so to the norms of justice. In this sense the value of law is objective while the value of justice is subjective."[69]

This view of justice, as already noted, is part of a larger view that sees value, good, and the whole range of moral terms as sharply set against fact and reason. Any judgment that is normative, as declaring that such-and-such should or ought to be done, is by that very fact classified as nonrational, if not irrational. What is normative, in this sense, is held to be removed from the sphere of the objective and the rational.

Thus, even if justice should have some objective reference (contrary to the position of Ross and Kelsen), it still is held that this would not affect the normative character of justice. Stevenson, for example, maintains that justice, in common with some other ethical terms, contains both a descriptive and an emotive meaning. A statement of the form "This is just" can be analyzed as having "the meaning of 'This has the qualities or relations X, Y, Z . . .'" which may be

[67] *Op. cit.*, p. 6.
[68] *Ibid.*, p. 49.
[69] *Ibid.*; cf. p. 14.

descriptive and objective and "have something to do with the distribution of commodities or opportunities or with equality, or with law, etc." But in addition to this descriptive meaning, "just" also has "a laudatory emotive meaning which permits it to express the speaker's approval and tends to evoke the approval of the hearer."[70]

Furthermore, and this is now the important point, it is the persuasive part of the definition, and not the objective descriptive part, that carries the normative and specifically ethical load of the term. To single out one descriptive meaning, say, equality or law, as providing the essence of justice is to become evaluative, Stevenson writes, and to plead a moral cause; it is to make what he calls a persuasive definition, aimed at persuading one to accept that view of justice.[71]

Stevenson thus agrees with Ross and Kelsen in holding that justice as normative is emotive and not objective, and, if not actually irrational, still involves more than reason. It is important to note, however, that Stevenson is not an adherent of the Positive Law position on justice. He does not say that justice, when not normative, is equivalent to legality. As is evident from the passage just quoted, he says that the descriptive meaning of justice may consist in legality, equality, or something else, without himself settling for any one of these. In fact, Stevenson in what he has to say about justice is concerned to show what an adequate analysis of justice must do, rather than trying to do it himself: it must spell out the descriptive as well as the persuasive parts of the definition, as Stevenson calls them, and this is something that he does not attempt.

Although Stevenson is not himself an adherent of the Positive Law theory of justice, his analysis is important for understanding that theory. It confirms the contention that the theory consists essentially of two parts—one positive and the other negative. The positive part, which Stevenson calls descriptive, consists in the identification of justice with legality. But this very identification adds to the notion of legality what Stevenson calls the laudatory note, which is absent from

---

[70] *Ethics and Language*, pp. 207, 221. In this quoted passage, I have put the word "just" where Stevenson has "good." This is warranted by Stevenson's statement on p. 237 that "what has been said of 'good' might have been said of any other ethical term, and indeed, of any term that is subject to persuasive definition," and "just" is cited and analyzed by Stevenson as a term that is typical of "persuasive definition." Furthermore, in his 1938 articles in *Mind* on persuasive definition (pp. 345–349), Stevenson takes the expression "This is just" as paradigm for the analysis that he develops later in his book, with the example, "This is good."

[71] See *ibid.*, pp. 221–223.

the meaning of legality as such: it introduces what we have been calling the approbative factor. The negative part of the theory is accordingly concerned with showing that justice in any other sense than that of legality must amount to nothing more than an expression of approval. In other words, the Positive Law theory maintains that justice divorced from legality loses all descriptive meaning and becomes approbative only.

We have distinguished and identified two fundamental characteristics of justice on the Positive Law theory. (1) As referring to positive law, justice implies a norm of social action which is objective. It is a relational notion, implying the existence of many individuals engaged in some kind of common action. But (2) as approbative and implying that action which conforms to the norm is good, justice is subjective and relative to the individual. What is unique about the theory, which distinguishes it from the other basic theories, is its tendency to isolate these two elements and provide them with distinct explanations.

THE OBLIGATORINESS OF JUSTICE

To say that X is just is to indicate approval of X, that X is good, but it also implies that X ought to be done. But why ought one be just? Since the Positive Law theory identifies justice with legality, the question amounts to asking—Why ought one to obey the law?

The answer of the Positive Law theory to these questions about obligatoriness follows from the position it has already taken regarding the preceding issues. Since justice has been identified with legality, it has behind it all the might of the law. But, since justice is also held to involve subjective approbation, it also enjoys the sanction of personal approval. Thus to the question, what kind of *ought* is involved in justice, the Positive Law theory provides a two-part answer. There is, first, a punitive *ought,* founded on the physical sanction of the law, which may be expressed thus: I ought to do X, because if I do not, I will be punished. Second, there is what might be called an approbative *ought:* I ought to do X because it is something I approve of.

Hobbes again provides the clearest case. As we have already seen (above, p. 47), he maintains that "before the names of just and unjust can have place there must be some coercive power to compel men equally to the performance of their covenants by the terror of some punishment greater than the benefit they expect by the breach of their covenant."[72] Without the sanction of force, covenants are "but words and breath," and of themselves "have no force to oblige, contain, constrain, or protect any man."[73] From this it would appear that justice rests upon might.

Yet Hobbes also asserts that there is "no obligation on any man which arises not from some act of his own."[74] Every man has given his approval and agreed to the law by which he is governed: "The law is made by the sovereign power, and all that is done by such power is warranted and owned by every one of the people; and that which every man will have so, no man can say is unjust. It is in the laws of a commonwealth as in the laws of gaming: whatsoever the gamesters all agree on is injustice to none of them."[75] Hence, although justice for the Positive Law theory rests on might, it is also held to be based on the approval and agreement of the men who live under it.

The relation of force and agreement constitutes the crux of the problem for the Positive Law theory, and it is by bringing the two together that it explains the obligatoriness of justice. Plato's *Republic* supplies the classical locus for this explanation in the development given by Glaucon to the argument first advanced by Thrasymachus.

According to Thrasymachus, justice is nothing but "the interest of the stronger" (338c). Power, he claims, "is in every state in the hands of the ruling class, which makes laws in its own interest, a democracy making democratic laws, a tyranny tyrannical ones, and so on." The stronger and ruling powers "in making these laws defines as just for their subjects what is to the interest of themselves, and if anyone breaks their laws, he is punished for violation of justice" (338d-e). Thrasymachus, accordingly, claims that the just is the same in all states, namely, "the interest of the established ruling class," which he insists, is identical with "the interest of the stronger" (339a).

In making this claim, Thrasymachus stresses the dependence of justice upon power. It is the stronger who assert their will in the laws of the society they govern and thereby determine what is to count as just or unjust, that is, what should be done or avoided. They possess and exercise power over others, or, what Hobbes calls, a common power, and use it to compel obedience to their laws.

[72] *Op. cit.*, p. 110.
[73] *Ibid.*, p. 135.
[74] *Ibid.*, p. 166.
[75] *Ibid.*, p. 100.

Glaucon agrees with Thrasymachus that men would like to be strong enough to do anything they want to do without retaliation. They desire their own advantage and more than their share (*pleonexia*) (359c). But they are too weak, Glaucon claims, to succeed in their wish. They have learned from experience what it is to do wrong and to suffer it, and they have found that suffering wrong outweighs the good of inflicting it (358c). Consequently, men have made a compact with one another, neither to do nor to suffer wrong. "They make laws and covenants and what the law establishes they call lawful and just (*nominon kai dikaion*)" (359a). Such, Glaucon says, is "the origin and nature of justice." It is a compromise, or as he puts it, "justice lies midway between what is most desirable, *i.e.*, to do wrong and avoid punishment, and what is most undesirable, to suffer wrong without redress" (359b).

As is apparent from Glaucon's actual statement, he develops his position in terms of man's "natural desires." This can give rise to varying interpretations. The difficulty stems for the most part from the fact that Plato uses the one word "*dikaion*" indifferently for "just," "good," and "right." If we were to retain the one word "just" and its cognates for all occurrences of "*dikaion*" and its cognates in Glaucon's argument, we would find him asserting something like this:

> Men naturally desire to do injustice to others, and not to have injustice done to them. But, since men, individually, are too weak to secure these, they have agreed to surrender both and to establish laws governing their actions. These laws determine what is lawful and just.

From this it might appear that Glaucon is maintaining that there is both a natural and a conventional justice or injustice. Men "naturally desire more than their share," which is "naturally unjust," but this is restrained and controlled through the imposition of law, which establishes what is conventionally just or unjust. On this interpretation, Glaucon would not be advocating the Positive Law theory. Such an interpretation, however, ignores the ambiguities of "*dikaion*," which may mean what is morally good or right as well as what is legally just. Recognizing these ambiguities, one could claim that Glaucon, in talking about men naturally desiring "injustice," is referring to moral wrongness, whereas, in speaking of the work of law, he is referring to justice. Thus, it is not inaccurate to take "*dikaion*" in one place as "good" and in another as "just." To do so would point up the Positive

Law interpretation of his argument, which appears in his explicit statement that law determines the "lawful and just."

Glaucon claims that his argument revives or resumes that begun by Thrasymachus (358c). In our terms, this amounts to an admission that he adheres to the Positive Law theory. Yet Glaucon seems to differ with Thrasymachus about both the origin of law and also about the motive for obeying it. Thrasymachus would apparently trace both to the mere existence of superior force, whereas Glaucon argues the need for a common agreement. Such an agreement provides a motive for obedience on the part of those making it. If Glaucon is understood as implying that it also gives rise to a superior force, his argument would bring together both agreement and might as the underlying ground for obligation.

It may be doubted whether Glaucon is asserting such a position. But there is no doubt about Hobbes, since he makes clearly explicit the union of agreement and might as supplying the sanction of law and, hence, too, of justice. He develops his position in terms of the traditional terminology of natural law, but this usage, as we have already had occasion to observe, is verbal only and does not make him any less an adherent of the Positive Law theory.

Hobbes declares, as noted before (p. 60), that justice follows from the first two of what he calls "laws of nature." It would thus seem that the obligatoriness of justice somehow derives from them. The first law states that "every man ought to endeavor peace as far as he has hope of obtaining it."[76] The second declares "that a man be willing, when others are so too, as far forth as for peace and defense of himself he shall think it necessary, to lay down this right to all things, and be contented with so much liberty against other men as he would allow other men against himself."[77] The third law, "the fount and original of justice," requires "that men perform their covenants made,"[78] which is equivalent to requiring obedience to the sovereign and his law. The first two, as underlying the third, must somehow supply a sanction for obeying the law.

Why then ought one obey the law? What kind of *ought* is this on the basis of the first two laws? The first directs man to peace. By the second, he turns over his liberty and power to the sovereign as essen-

[76] *Ibid.*
[77] *Ibid.*
[78] *Ibid.*, p. 110.

tial to obtain peace. Clearly then, he ought to obey the sovereign power because only by so doing will he obtain peace. The *ought* involved is hypothetical and can be formulated thus: *If you want peace, you ought to obey the law.*

Against this, it might be argued that the first law, which also contains an *ought,* appeals to another kind which is not merely hypothetical but categorical and moral: in other words, that men naturally recognize peace is a good that ought to be pursued and that they would be wrong not to pursue. Hobbes does indeed seem to hold that men have a natural inclination toward peace, which is what he means, as we have seen, by calling it a "natural law." Yet this fact does not make peace a moral good that ought to be pursued. In fact, Hobbes says expressly that "words of good, evil, and contemptible are ever used with relation to the person that uses them, there being nothing simply and absolutely so; nor any common rule of good and evil to be taken from the nature of the objects themselves; but from the person of the man, where there is no commonwealth, or, in a commonwealth, from the person who represents it."[79] Man, then, considered apart from society, is not bound to pursue peace except as he desires it as a private good. The *ought* involved is again hypothetical: *If you want that, you ought to do this.* Hobbes's laws of nature are thus neither moral nor categorical, but individual and hypothetical as dictating the means needed to achieve a desired end.

Men acting in accordance with these "laws" enter the social compact, and this, for Hobbes, founds the commonwealth with all its superior and sovereign power (see above, pp. 47–48). The agreement of men produces the power, then, that suffices, in the ordinary civil state in which men live, to enforce obedience to its laws. Apart from agreement and might, there is no need for a distinct kind of moral obligation.

Might figures so prominently in the Positive Law account of the obligatoriness of justice that the theory is often accused by its opponents of confusing the two. Of course, Thrasymachus flatly declares that might is right, but his saying is suspect as the expression of a "straw man," erected only to be shot at. Positive Law adherents speaking for themselves frequently deny the proposition explicitly. Hobbes declares that it is false that "justice is but a vain word" and

79 *Ibid.,* p. 41.

that success makes right.[80] Austin, after noting that the proposition is "a great favorite with shallow scoffers and buffoons," writes that " 'right is might' . . . is either a flat truism affectedly and darkly expressed, or is thoroughly false and absurd."[81] It is false and absurd, he claims, if it is taken to mean either that might and right are the same thing or that a person possesses a right through his own power. "But if it means that every right is a creature of might or power it is merely a triusm disguised in paradoxical language. For every right—divine, legal, or moral—rests on a relative duty; that is to say, a duty lying on a party or parties other than the party or parties in whom the right resides. And, manifestly, that relative duty would not be a duty substantially if the law which affects to impose it were not sustained by might."[82]

But, of course, it is this very assertion of the dependence of duty, taken "substantially," upon might, that leads opponents of the theory to claim that right is confused with might. It appears to reduce the sanction of right and law to nothing but might. So, too, does Hobbes's claim that God holds His dominion over men by natural right because His "power is irresistible."[83]

The sanction behind the law, and hence also behind justice, is not for the Positive Law theory merely brute physical force. There are social sanctions in addition to the use of police power. Thus, Alf Ross claims that "most people obey the law, not only out of fear of the police or of extra-legal sanctions, but also from disinterested respect for the law." They develop what Ross calls an "institutional legal consciousness," which, he emphasizes, is not necessarily moral at all.[84] In claiming that this respect for the law is not moral, he means that it is a social habit or convention.

The Positive Law theory maintains that ultimately the only obligation or binding power of justice is legal force and social approval. It denies that there is any other kind of *ought*—any special moral *ought*—involved in justice. Questions of approval and of force are matters of fact: Is there or is there not approval for such-and-such? Is effective force available, and can it be applied in such-and-such a case? These are questions that are decidable, at least in principle, by

80 *Ibid.*, p. 227.
81 *Op cit.*, p. 285, note.
82 *Ibid.*
83 *Loc. cit.*
84 *Op. cit.*, pp. 54–55.

consulting the state of affairs in a given society. There is no need to appeal to any other kind of understanding of what ought to be done. Hence, the theory tends to deny that there is any sharp distinction or division between *isness* and *oughtness*. Thus, Holmes, writing to Laski, says: "I do accept 'a rough equation between *isness* and *oughtness*,' or rather I don't know anything about oughtness except Cromwell's—'a few poor gentlemen have put their lives upon it.' I also would fight for some things, but instead of saying they ought to be, I merely say they are part of the kind of world that I like, or should like."[85] In this passage, the three notes characteristic of the position on the normativeness of justice are brought together: subjective preference, power (that he would "fight for" it), and the denial of any special or peculiar moral *ought*.

The concern to avoid a moral *ought* appears strongly in Hobbes. He claims that injustice amounts to a contradiction: "Injury or injustice in the controversies of the world is somewhat like to that which in the disputations of scholars is called absurdity. For as it is there called an absurdity to contradict what one maintained in the beginning, so in the world it is called injustice and injury voluntarily to undo that which from the beginning he had voluntarily done."[86] But what one "had voluntarily done," on Hobbes's theory of the social contract, is to renounce any individual power to govern in favor of the establishment of a common power. In effect, Hobbes claims that we have given our promise, and not to keep it is to unsay it. Thus justice and injustice are compared to saying and unsaying the same thing. The obligation of keeping a promise is reduced to the fact of having given a promise, and any appeal to an extraneous principle, such as that promises ought to be kept, is avoided.

The Virtue of Justice: Obedience

From considering why the law ought to be obeyed, we have obtained the answer of the Positive Law theory to the question, why one ought to be just. Law itself, as we have seen from analysis of the theory, provides the only objective norm of justice. It lays down what actions must be done or avoided if one is to be just, and its sanctions ensure obedience. If, then, we ask who the just man is, and what kind

[85] *Holmes-Laski Letter,* June 1, 1927, p. 948.
[86] *Op. cit.,* p. 101.

of character he has, we should expect to find that the Positive Law theory identifies him with the obedient man.

This conclusion with regard to justice as a virtue is implicit in the Positive Law position. Yet it is seldom stated explicitly. For the most part, the Positive Law authors say nothing at all about justice as a virtue. But, when they do, they do so to counter the claim that justice is a distinctive virtue separate from all others. Hobbes is a case in point and an interesting one in that at first sight he seems to be identifying justice with something different from obedience, which, to say the least, would be upsetting in an author taken as paradigm for the Positive Law position. The discrepancy, however, is only apparent and the result of connecting the theory of justice with a social contract account of government and society.

Hobbes contends, as we have seen (p. 60), that the basis of justice lies in the injunction "that men perform their covenants made," so that "the definition of injustice is no other than the not performance of covenant." From this, Hobbes might appear to be saying that justice consists in keeping one's word, and not in obedience to the law. But this would be a misinterpretation. He does hold that justice consists in keeping one's word, but for him this action is identical with obeying the law. For the covenant in question is ultimately the original compact establishing Leviathan under which a man agrees to obey his sovereign's commands, and these comprise the positive law.

The emphasis upon the "keeping of covenant" obviously derives from the social contract theory of law and not from the theory of justice as conformity to law. But the social contract is not essential to the Positive Law position on justice, and it is possible to adhere to the latter without asserting the social contract. Both Austin and Kelsen repudiate and even ridicule the notion of any explicit contract underlying civil society. Some amount of common agreement and acceptance of rules for social behavior is admittedly necessary, but they see no reason for describing this need as contract or compact. Hence, in facing the issue of justice as a virtue, we must express the position of the Positive Law theory in such a way as not to commit one to a social compact theory of law. That position must be formulated so that it would be claimed by both those who hold a social contract theory and those who deny it. This is accomplished by characterizing the virtue of justice as consisting in obedience. Not only would Hobbes ascribe to this proposition, but so, too, would Austin and Kelsen.

Hobbes's account of justice as a virtue is special in still another respect, which derives from his equating justice with a "law of nature." By this, as we have seen, he does not mean at all what the Natural Law theorists mean by the term (cf. above, pp. 59, 71). Hobbes claims that "the justice of manners is that which is meant where justice is called a virtue and injustice a vice."[87] Distinguishing "manners or manner of life" from actions, he notes that "the names of just and unjust, when they are attributed to men, signify one thing, and when they are attributed to actions, another." When applied to manners, "injustice is but the disposition or aptitude to do injury and is injustice before it proceed to act and without supposing any individual person injured."[88] So, too, in applying the terms to men, he notes that "a just man . . . is he that taketh all the care he can that his actions may be all just, and an unjust man is he that neglects it." In other words, Hobbes is pointing out the dispositional function of the terms when they are applied to men and manners.

In all this there is nothing exceptional. But when he comes to describe the justice of men and manners, he identifies it with "conformity or inconformity to reason,"[89] and not with the disposition to keep one's covenant or to obey the law. But again we should not be surprised since for Hobbes all three terms are intimately connected. As we have seen before, it is both natural and reasonable, according to Hobbes, that men submit to a sovereign in order to escape the war of all against all in the state of nature. Justice, he writes, "that is to say, keeping of covenant, is a rule of reason by which we are forbidden to do anything destructive to our life, and consequently, a law of nature."[90] But keeping the covenant consists in obeying the sovereign law. Hence, all three terms are brought together into one: keeping the covenant, obeying the law, and conforming to reason. Although he uses the prescriptive language of morals (we are "forbidden to do anything"), the obligation, as we saw from his account of the obligatoriness of justice, is hypothetical and not moral and categorical. No social rules of morality exist until the sovereign law is promulgated, since the laws themselves constitute the rules of good and evil.

Justice is a virtue for Hobbes, and he writes of it as a disposition to

[87] *Ibid.*, p. 114.
[88] *Ibid.*
[89] *Ibid.*
[90] *Ibid.*, p. 113.

act in a certain way, a manner of life, coming from performing many just acts, and one that is not lost or destroyed "by one or a few unjust actions that proceed from sudden passion or mistake of things or persons."[91] But the way that he characterizes this disposition is special and peculiar to his social contract theory. To reformulate his position so as to make it acceptable to any adherent of the Positive Law theory, we need only say that justice as a virtue consists in the disposition to perform acts that are in conformity with the positive law of the land. So formulated, it expresses a position about justice as a virtue that is characteristic of the Positive Law theory of justice.

With this we have completed our construction of the Positive Law theory. Law, or legality, is the privileged term of the theory. It can be said that the main characteristic of the theory is the identification of justice with legality. But to be faithful to the theory and accurate in expressing its main position, this statement must always be understood with the qualification that justice is being taken only in a determinate and objective sense. The theory maintains that legality constitutes the only determinate and objective meaning of justice. It does not deny that justice is used in other senses. But it does maintain that, when justice is used to mean something different from legality, the meaning is indeterminate and subjective. It may be revealing something about the speaker; it is not asserting anything about the world. It is indicating that the speaker approves of the object he calls just, that he thinks it good, perhaps even that he would defend it; but it does not signify anything about the object itself. Only when justice means legality does it say something determinate and objective about its object, for it then refers to a definite system of law with objective and determinate rules of procedure.

Of course, much more could be said about the theory, but we now have what we need to compare and contrast it with the other major theories of justice. We have determined its position on each of the six fundamental issues that give rise to major controversy. The position taken by the Positive Law theory can be summarized in brief by collecting the principal propositions of our construction. These constitute what might be thought of as the identifying propositions of the theory.

[91] *Ibid.,* p. 114.

(1) Justice and injustice are dependent on positive law.
   Where there is no law there is no justice.
   Justice depends on society and varies according to the constitution of the society.

(2) Law itself is independent of justice.
   Law is not just or unjust.
   The pursuit of justice is not the purpose of law.
   No state as such is just or unjust.

(3) Justice consists in conformity to the positive law.
   Justice is not adequately defined as rendering to each his due.
   Justice is not based on natural right.

(4) Justice apart from legality is merely a subjective norm.
   Justice implies approbation as well as legality.
   The approbation of justice, apart from legality, is subjective.

(5) Justice is obligatory ultimately only because of legal sanctions.
   The sanction of law and hence of justice rests on agreement and might.
   Justice imposes no distinct kind of moral duty.

(6) The virtue of justice is identical with obedience.

5

The Social Good Theory of Justice

T H E following six propositions serve to identify the Social Good theory of justice:

(1) Justice and injustice are not exclusively dependent on positive law.
(2) Justice provides a criterion for the goodness of a law.
(3) Justice derives exclusively from society and consists ultimately in promoting the social good.
(4) Justice is an objective norm for human actions.
(5) Justice imposes a moral duty based on the social good and is not primarily dependent on legal sanctions.
(6) Justice is a distinct virtue, disposing one to act for the social good, and is similar to benevolence.

Each of the six propositions asserts a definite position regarding the corresponding fundamental issue. On some of the issues the position asserted is the same as that taken by the Natural Right theory and is opposed to that taken by the Positive Law theory of justice. Yet there is no assertion of natural right as such, and, in the exposition of the third proposition, we shall see that it is explicitly denied that natural right provides the basis of justice. In fact, the explicit reference to the social good in the third, fifth, and sixth propositions serves to distinguish this theory from the Natural Right theory of justice.

In addition to its denial of natural right, the theory shares still another feature with the Positive Law theory. It takes the same position on the relation between justice and society. All theories agree that justice is a social norm and applies only to men in their social relations. But unlike the Natural Right theory, and in opposition to it, these two theories hold further that society is the sole source of justice and arises only from the agreements men make in order to promote their social life. It denies that justice has a natural basis and thus, in effect, holds that it is basically a conventional relation. While at first sight it may appear that the Social Good theory sharply opposes the Positive Law theory on each of the six fundamental issues, this is actually not the case. On the third issue, regarding natural right and the relation of justice to society, the two theories agree in affirming the conventional basis of justice.

On the other issues, however, the theory departs from the Positive Law theory and agrees with the Natural Right theory. It refuses to limit justice to questions of positive law (1), allows expressly that justice is a criterion of law (2), that it is an objective norm (4), that it has its own special moral sanction attaching to its dictates (5), and that it is a distinct virtue (6).

Even if the theory did no more than combine certain assertions of the Positive Law theory with other assertions from the Natural Right theory, it would still constitute a distinct position. In fact, it does more than this. Not only does the Social Good theory assert certain propositions that are uniquely its own, but, since these happen to lie at the very heart of its position, they also affect the interpretation of those propositions it holds in common with the other two basic positions. It agrees with the Natural Right theory, for example, in holding that justice can provide a criterion for law: If a law is unjust, it is to that extent a bad law. But if we ask what it means for a law to be unjust, we receive very different answers from the two theories. The one can claim that a law is unjust because it has violated a natural right—an answer that the Social Good theory would not allow. On this theory, the injustice of a law must result ultimately, not from relation to any supposed natural right but from the fact that it goes counter to the social good of the group whose law it is. The fact that two theories may express general agreement with regard to one of the fundamental issues does not mean that they do so for the same reasons.

PROPONENTS OF THE SOCIAL GOOD THEORY

Baylis	Mill
Bentham	Moore
Blanshard	Pound
Broad	Radbruch
Godwin	Rashdall
Hobhouse	Rawls
Hume	Sidgwick
Ihering*	Smith
Lloyd	Toulmin
Melden	

* A dialectically difficult author. See above, p. 22.

The same qualifications that were used in categorizing the Positive Law authors apply here. The Social Good theory identified by the six propositions is a dialectical construction, and a writer is counted as a proponent of it if his theory of justice approaches it as a limit or an ideal. All that is claimed is that his writing on justice provides ground for declaring that he would assert each of the six identifying propositions of the theory.

The inclusion of Bentham, Mill, and Sidgwick in the list shows that the theory of justice with which we are now concerned was that held by the classical Utilitarian philosophers. For this reason, it is tempting to call it the Utilitarian theory of justice. Yet to do so would be seriously misleading. There are men on the list—Blanshard, to name only one—who would object to the name, since they would deny either that the social good consists in the greatest good of the greatest number or that pleasure constitutes the only good desirable for itself. Furthermore, there are writers who would be counted as Utilitarians for holding these two positions and yet who would not accept this theory of justice: Austin is an example, since, as we have seen, he holds the Positive Law theory.

Consequently, for the sake of accuracy, it is better not to name the theory after the Utilitarians, even though it still remains true that the classical Utilitarian philosophers provide the paradigm case of the theory. The writings of Hume, Mill, and Sidgwick are accordingly cited extensively in the documentation of the position. As already noted, the Social Good position falls to some extent between the Positive Law and the Natural Right theories of justice, and shares something with both. The same distribution is found among the three authors taken as paradigm cases of the position. Hume's theory of justice is in many respects close to the Positive Law position, especially in his account of justice as a sentiment. In fact, Sidgwick classifies him with those who identify justice with law observance.[1] This would seem to make him an adherent of the Positive Law theory, although, as will be seen, the balance of evidence is against this classification. Sidgwick's account of justice, on many issues, approaches that of the Natural Right theory. Mill would thus appear to be left in the middle and, hence, the most paradigmatic of the Social Good position as such. But this is not quite borne out. All three authors are needed for the full statement of the position, since one is better and clearer than another on certain of the fundamental issues.

In constructing the Social Good theory of justice, I will follow the same method that I used in constructing the Positive Law theory. I will formulate in my own language the propositions that serve to identify the theory and the acceptance of which serves to indicate that one is a proponent of it. I will provide documentation to show that the positions asserted in the identifying propositions have in fact been taken in the literature on justice and indicate some of the leading arguments advanced for holding those positions. In the course of doing these things, there also will be occasion to note the way in which the Social Good theory differs from the other basic positions regarding justice, although full discussion of these differences is reserved for Chapter 7.

THE INDEPENDENCE OF JUSTICE FROM LAW

The way in which the Social Good theory differs from the Positive Law theory is most apparent, of course, from what it has to say about the relation between justice and law. Unlike that theory, it refuses to identify justice with conformity to the positive law.

Sidgwick speaks for all proponents of the Social Good position when he claims that "reflection shows that we do not mean by justice

[1] *Methods of Ethics,* p. 440.

merely conformity to law." For this claim, he cites three reasons: "First, we do not always call the violators of the law unjust, but only of some laws: not, for example, duellists or gamblers. And, secondly, we often judge that law as it exists does not completely realize justice; our notion of justice furnishes a standard with which we compare actual laws, and pronounce them just or unjust. And, thirdly, there is a part of just conduct which lies outside the sphere of law as it ought to be; for example, we think that a father may be just or unjust to his children in matters where the law leaves (and ought to leave) him free."[2]

Sidgwick's first reason confines itself to the area covered by law and claims that failure to conform to the law does not always, by that very fact, make one unjust. The second looks to the law itself and claims that justice provides a standard for it. The third looks beyond the law to an area where law does not, and should not, apply and yet where justice is still relevant. The three reasons suffice, according to the Social Good theory, to show that justice is a wider notion than law and transcends it.

Social Good authors do not always make all three of Sidgwick's points, and I do not know whether all would accept the first of them as valid. All, however, would assert the second and third. Mill, for example, asserts that "mankind considers the idea of justice and its obligations as applicable to many things which neither are, nor is it desired that they should be, regulated by law." Among these he mentions in particular the details of private life. "Nobody desires that laws should interfere with the whole detail of private life," he writes. "Yet everyone allows that in all daily conduct a person may and does show himself to be either just or unjust."[3]

The standards of justice we appeal to in our private life are not confined to that sphere. They also may be used in more public matters without involving any reference to law. "It is universally considered just," Mill writes, "that each person should obtain that (whether good or evil) which he *deserves;* and unjust that he should obtain a good, or be made to undergo an evil, which he does not deserve. . . . It is confessedly unjust to *break faith* with anyone: to violate an engagement either express or implied, or disappoint expectations raised by our own conduct, at least if we have raised those expectations know-

[2] *Ibid.*, p. 265.
[3] *Utilitarianism*, pp. 58–59.

ingly and voluntarily. . . . It is by universal admission inconsistent
with justice to be *partial;* to show favor or preference to one person
over another, in matters to which favor and preference do not properly
apply."[4] In none of these senses is justice dependent upon positive
law, Mill claims, and cases can be imagined in which one could use
justice in one or another of them without making any reference to
law.

The Positive Law theory denies that there is such a thing as a
"natural justice," separate and distinct from the norm of justice
established by positive law. The adherents of the Social Good theory,
however, find nothing wrong in such a notion. Both Mill and Hume
use the expression "natural justice." Hume does so in the course of
taking issue with Hobbes regarding the contrast between the natural
and the civil.

Hume argues against Hobbes that there is such a thing as "natural
justice," if by this one understands the justice proper to a condition of
society without civil government and positive law. For Hume, unlike
Hobbes, both society and justice precede government, and "the state
of society without government" is not only conceivable, but it is also
"one of the most natural states of men."[5] In this state, contrary to
Hobbes, justice is absolutely necessary. "Though it be possible for
men to maintain a small uncultivated society without government, 'tis
impossible," Hume writes, "they should maintain a society of any kind
without justice."[6] In other words, justice is necessary for society and is
presupposed by government and politically organized society, or by
what Hume calls "civil society." Hence, distinct from civil society
with its laws and its justice, there is for Hume a "natural code" and a
"natural justice."[7]

For the Social Good theory, positive law is not constitutive of
justice. In fact, justice itself, that is "natural justice," provides a
criterion for judging the goodness of positive law. When laws become
"so perverse as to cross all interests of society," Hume declares that
they then lose all authority, and "men judge by ideas of natural
justice." So, too, Mill discusses the "repartition of Taxation" in terms
of "natural justice."[8] The Social Good authors maintain that laws

4 *Ibid.,* pp. 54–55.
5 *A Treatise of Human Nature,* p. 501.
6 *Ibid.,* p. 541.
7 *Enquiry Concerning the Principles of Morals,* pp. 196–197, note.
8 *Op. cit.,* p. 72.

themselves may be just or unjust. Opinions may differ "as to the justice or injustice of infringing" a law, but, Mill claims, "it seems to be universally admitted that there may be unjust laws, and that law, consequently, is not the ultimate criterion of justice."[9]

Justice, for the Social Good theory, is a wider notion than law. Even so, it still can maintain that men ordinarily first think of justice and come to know it in connection with law. Mill says that there can "be no doubt that the *idée mère,* the primitive element, in the formation of the notion of justice, was conformity to law." He writes, "in most, if not in all, languages the etymology of the word which corresponds to 'Just,' points distinctly to an origin connected with the ordinances of law. *Justum* is a form of *jussum,* that which has been ordered. *Dikaion* comes directly from *diké,* a suit at law. *Recht,* from which came *right* and *righteous,* is synonymous with law."[10]

Proponents of the Social Good position on justice may admit that conformity to the law is the first and best known instance of justice, the *idée mère,* as Mill says. But this of itself does not detract from the position or make it any less opposed to the Positive Law position. What is essential is the claim that law does not exhaust the notion of justice, and, in addition, that justice also provides a criterion for judging the law itself.

THE DEPENDENCE OF JUSTICE ON SOCIETY

On the issue regarding the relation between justice and law, the Social Good theory disagrees with the Positive Law theory and agrees with the Natural Right theory. Some of its adherents even talk, as we have seen, in terms of "natural justice." Yet the theory is not "naturalist" at all in the sense that the Natural Right theory is. The difference becomes manifest from the position it takes regarding the relation between justice and society.

The heart of the Social Good theory lies in the claim that all questions of justice must ultimately be decided in terms of social utility. All theories of justice agree that justice is a social norm that applies to men in their relations with one another. The Social Good theory goes still further and asserts that the origin and basis of justice lies in the good of society; that is, in a good greater than any indi-

9 *Ibid.,* p. 54.
10 *Ibid.,* pp. 57–58.

vidual or private good, achievable only through men acting in common, and one in which individuals can find their own good. Social Good authors may differ about the social good and its determination. But all would agree that what is just is ultimately decided only by determining what is good for society, and that, whenever a course of action definitely runs counter to that good, it is to that extent unjust. There is no law, no right that falls outside this criterion. All laws and rights are just or unjust according as they conform to the social good and promote it. Justice as a norm rests ultimately upon the social good.

According to the Social Good theory, justice is based entirely on society. It arises in the course of men striving to work out a common life, and, if it were possible for men to live apart from society, there would be no justice and no morality at all. Justice, like the morals of society, grows out of the mores of men. It is evolved by them through their efforts to meet the demands of living together. If the conventional is understood to refer to what is entirely the work of society without any natural basis, then the Social Good position is no less conventional than that of the Positive Law theory. But unlike this latter theory it maintains that society is logically prior to law as well as justice. The theory holds that, while it may make sense to speak of justice where there is no organized government and no positive law, justice makes no sense apart from the good of society.

This theory in its account of justice places emphasis upon the social situation of man and its needs, and not upon man as such in any social situation. The sociality, so to speak, that gives rise to justice is a property of special conditions, not a property belonging in any way to man as such. An individual is in no way naturally just. He is made just by and in society, and all the rights and the rules of justice are entirely made by and conferred by society. The theory holds, accordingly, that there is no natural right, as such, underlying justice and its duties.

Adherents of the Social Good theory assert the dependence of justice upon society in different ways. Hume does so by claiming that justice is an "artificial," not a "natural, virtue." Mill accomplishes the same purpose by tracing the origin of justice to a social feeling. Sidgwick denies that natural right affords a basis for justice. All three arguments are equivalent in asserting the dependence of justice upon society and denying its dependence upon natural right. This position constitutes the major source of difference from the Natural Right theory and also leads to all that is most characteristic of the Social Good theory of justice as such.

According to Hume, justice is an "artificial virtue." Unlike benevolence or the feeling of sympathy we have for our fellowmen, justice is not a "simple original instinct,"[11] an "innate idea," or an "instinct originally implanted in our nature."[12] For this claim, Hume marshals a variety of reasons, but two principal ones can be distinguished: one from the nature of property, and the other from what might be called the systematic character of justice.

Property, for Hume, constitutes "the object of justice." If justice is natural, then, he argues, there must also be a "simple original instinct" for property. "But who is there that ever heard of such an instinct?" Hume asks.[13] The rights that characterize property are too numerous to be natural; they do not admit of degree, as natural feelings do; and they are often contrary to the common feelings of humanity.[14] On these grounds, Hume concludes that the sense of justice cannot be natural, but must be artificial, or contrived by man—not innate, but acquired. It arises from reflection upon social experience and seeing what is needed for men to live together. Only by looking at the whole network of social relations can we understand, Hume claims, where justice lies. A single act of a "natural virtue," such as benevolence, shows its goodness immediately; we see that it is good to help a fellowman in distress. But a single act of justice, Hume claims, may frequently appear neither good nor just when considered in itself, apart from the larger framework within which it occurs. "Judges take from a poor man to give to a rich; they bestow on the dissolute the labor of the industrious; and put into the hands of the vicious the means of harming both themselves and others." If we separate such judgments from the social fabric to which they belong, Hume claims "it would as often be an instance of humanity to decide contrary to the laws of justice as conformable to them." It is only when we look to the whole social scheme that we find such instances "advantageous to society." This feature of justice, according to Hume, at once distinguishes justice from a natural virtue such as benevolence. "When I relieve persons in distress, my natural humanity is my motive; and so

[11] *Op. cit.*, p. 201.
[12] *A Treatise of Human Nature*, p. 417.
[13] *Enquiry Concerning the Principles of Morals*, p. 201.
[14] See *A Treatise of Human Nature*, pp. 526–533.

far as my succor extends, so far have I promoted the happiness of my
fellow-creatures."[15] The goodness of benevolence is evident in every
single act, and there is no need to look beyond it to a whole system of
relations. That we must do so in the case of justice, Hume takes as
showing that justice is an artificial and not a natural virtue.

Hume employs still another argument to show the dependence of
justice upon society, which leads into the kind of analysis both Mill
and Sidgwick make. If justice were natural to man, independent of his
special social situation, then we could expect to find justice wherever
we find man. Yet Hume contends that it is easy to imagine situations
in which justice would not exist since there would be no need for it.
Of this he offers several examples: the golden age of the poets, where
men enjoy an abundance of all they want; a society of saints, where
every man has perfect benevolence; a condition of such extreme
indigence that there is not enough to prevent most of its members
from starving; a society of ruffians; Hobbes's state of nature, that is, a
society in which there is "no degree of equality"; or the condition of a
solitary man who has everything. In any and all of these situations,
Hume maintains that there would be no question of justice at all since
there would be no function for it to perform.[16]

The need for justice, according to Hume, arises only from the
special situation in which man finds himself. "The rules of equity or
justice," he writes, "depend entirely on the particular condition in
which men are placed."[17] Man has been loaded by nature with
"numberless wants and necessities" at the same time that he has been
supplied with but the slenderest means of relieving them. Left to
himself, he faces all but certain ruin and misery. "His force is too
small to execute any considerable work," his labor is so dissipated in
satisfying his many different needs that "he never attains a perfection
in any particular art," and he constantly faces ruin from the least
failure in either his strength or his art. Furthermore, men are naturally partial to themselves, and, with the natural scarcity of material
goods, they are only too prone to seize whatever they can for the
private use of themselves and their families. Self-interest, however,
does not blind man to where his self-interest actually lies. Even
though no other passion is naturally strong enough to overbear the

[15] *Ibid.*, p. 579.
[16] *Enquiry Concerning the Principles of Morals*, pp. 183–192.
[17] *Ibid.*, p. 188.

"interested affection," it is capable of being controlled by "an alteration of direction," and, according to Hume "this alteration must
necessarily take place upon the least reflection."[18]

In this reflection of man upon his condition and its amelioration,
Hume locates the origin and foundation of justice. The acquisitive
passions pose the great threat to a peaceable and secure life together,
but they can be brought under control by regularizing the possession
of the material goods that are their object. "This can be done," Hume
writes, "after no other manner than by a convention entered into by
all the members of society to bestow stability on the possession of
those external goods and leave everyone in the peaceable enjoyment of
what he may acquire by his fortune and industry."[19] Justice thus has
its origin in "a kind of convention or agreement, i.e. by a sense of
interest supposed to be common to all, and where every single act is
performed in expectation that others are to perform the like."[20]

Justice, then, is conventional, not natural. This is a position the
Social Good theory shares with the Positive Law theory in common
opposition to the Natural Right theory. It is important to note,
however, that it is not essential to the Social Good theory to identify
the conventional character of justice with an explicit social contract
theory of government. Not all Social Good authors would place as
much emphasis upon property as Hume does. But all would agree
with him in denying that the conventional character of justice rests
upon a promise. "Nothing can be more absurd," he declares. "The
observance of promises is itself one of the most considerable parts of
justice, and we are not surely bound to keep our word because we
have given our word to keep it." What Hume understands by a
convention, and here he is typical of all Social Good authors, is "a
sense of common interest, which sense each man feels in his own
breast, which he remarks in his fellows, and which carries him, in
concurrence with others, into a general plan or system of actions
which tends to public utility."[21]

Among the Social Good authors, Rawls is one of the few who finds
it useful to analyze justice in terms of an explicit contract. He asks us
to "imagine a number of rational and mutually self-interested persons
situated in an initial position of equal liberty" engaged in proposing

18 *A Treatise of Human Nature,* p. 484.
19 *Ibid.,* p. 489.
20 *Ibid.,* p. 498.
21 *Enquiry Concerning the Principles of Morals,* p. 306.

and acknowledging "before one another general principles applicable to their common institutions as standards by which their complaints against these institutions are to be judged." From this imaginary situation, Rawls claims to "derive" the basic principles of justice. For, in such a situation, he maintains that the following two principles would be acknowledged: "(i) Each person participating in the political and social system or affected by it has an equal right to the most extensive liberty compatible with a like liberty for all; and (ii) inequalities (as defined and permitted by the pattern of distribution of rights and duties) are arbitrary unless it is reasonable to expect that they will work out for everyone's advantage, and provided that the positions and offices to which they attach, or from which they may be gained, are open to all."[22]

The fact that Rawls conceives first of justice as a condition that must be accepted if men are to engage in a common enterprise is the main reason for assigning his theory to the Social Good position. It must be admitted that his theory is difficult to classify. He also holds that "the sense of justice" is one of the "fundamental attitudes and capacities included under the notion of humanity," which all men "originally possess."[23] In thus claiming that justice is natural to man, it might be argued that Rawls is better identified as an adherent of the Natural Right theory. Yet the fact that he makes the notion of contract central to his thought, even if only as an "analytical construction," shows that he is better placed with the Social Good authors. Rawls, like Hume, is an example of an author who can maintain that justice is natural in some sense without thereby leaving the Social Good position. What is essential is the subordination of justice to society in such a way that all its principles are made ultimately dependent upon that society and its needs. Rawls's use of the social contract would seem to satisfy this condition. In discussing justice, he maintains that we must view "each person as an individual sovereign," engaged in deciding with others how they are to lead a life together.[24]

The employment of the notion of a social contract as an analytical device does not by itself identify an author with any one of our three basic positions. Authors who use it can be found in all three. Hobbes,

[22] "The Sense of Justice," in *The Philosophical Review*, Vol. 72, 1963, pp. 283–284.
[23] *Ibid.*, pp. 299, 302.
[24] *Ibid.*, p. 304; cf. p. 282.

as we have seen, employs the social contract in developing his Positive Law theory of justice. Locke also uses the notion, as we will see, yet he advocates the Natural Right position. Rawls's use of it differs from both, however, in that he claims to "derive" the basic principles of justice from the social contract situation as implicit in it. For Hobbes, justice is posterior to law as well as to the social contract. For Locke, principles of justice exist even prior to the social contract. But for Rawls, they are implicit in the contract itself.

Mill does not declare as explicitly as Hume that justice is a social convention. Yet he clearly implies as much in the account he gives of the origin of justice. In his account he is mainly concerned with the source of the sanction of justice, that is, with its obligatoriness. Hence, most of what he has to say is more appropriate to the consideration of that issue. We are concerned now only with seeing how he makes justice depend upon society.

There are "two essential ingredients in the sentiment of justice," Mill claims, "the desire to punish a person who has done harm, and the knowledge or belief that there is some definite individual or individuals to whom harm has been done."[25] The desire to punish a person who has done harm he analyzes as "a spontaneous outgrowth from two sentiments . . . the impulse of self-defence and the feeling of sympathy."[26] He holds that "it is natural to resent, and to repel or retaliate any harm done or attempted against ourselves or against those with whom we sympathize." The desire to punish arises in us even when we are not ourselves the immediate object of injury. The purely self-regarding feeling is transcended or widened by sympathy and intelligence with the result that "a human being is capable of apprehending a community of interest between himself and the human society of which he forms a part, such that any conduct which threatens the security of the society generally, is threatening to his own, and calls forth his instinct (if instinct it be) of self-defence."[27]

Mill thus attributes to sympathy the function of socializing, as it were, the otherwise self-regarding feeling of self-defense and retaliation. Yet, in itself, at this stage, the feeling is still nonmoral; it "has nothing moral in it." As a "natural feeling," it makes us "resent indiscriminately whatever anyone does that is disagreeable to us." It

[25] *Op. cit.,* p. 62.
[26] *Ibid.,* p. 63.
[27] *Ibid.*

becomes moral only when there is "an exclusive subordination of it to the social sympathies, so as to wait on and obey their call." Mill says that the natural feeling is "moralized by the social feeling" when "it only acts in the directions conformable to the general good." We may be thinking only of the individual case when we feel our sentiment of justice outraged, and not thinking of society at large, or of any collective interest. But, according to Mill, "a person whose resentment is really a moral feeling, that is, who considers whether an act is blamable before he allows himself to resent it—such a person, though he may not say expressly to himself that he is standing up for the interest of society, certainly does feel that he is asserting a rule which is for the benefit of others as well as for his own. If he is not feeling this—if he is regarding the act solely as it affects him individually— he is not consciously just; he is not concerning himself about the justice of his actions.[28] Thus, for Mill, as for Hume, justice implies in itself and in its origin the "interest of society."

Although Rawls is critical of the classical Utilitarians, he still agrees with the Social Good position, as we have seen. Justice, he writes, supposes mutual recognition of principles by the participants in a common practice."[29] Questions about justice arise "when free persons who have no authority over each other are engaged in joint activity and settling rules which define it and determine shares in benefits and burdens.[30] It involves "acknowledgement of constraint required by fair play" and recognition that it is unfair "if one accepts benefit of practice but refuses to do his part in maintaining it."[31] Justice as fairness thus involves essentially the notion of social as opposed to antisocial behavior.

A. I. Melden shows his adherence to the Social Good theory by declaring that "it is self-evident—analytic—that it is right that one maintain the moral community of which one is a member. To be right is the very same thing as to be the kind of action that does serve, however that may be, the moral community."[32] What is right or moral, hence also what is just, is so precisely because it is necessary to the existence of the community."[33]

---

28 *Ibid.*, p. 64.
29 *Op. cit.*, p. 106.
30 *Ibid.*, p. 93.
31 *Ibid.*, pp. 95–96.
32 *Rights and Right Conduct*, p. 71.
33 See *ibid.*, pp. 76–77.

According to Roscoe Pound, justice is not an individual virtue, nor an ideal relation among men, but "such an adjustment of relations and ordering of conduct as will make the goods of existence . . . go round as far as possible with the least friction and waste."[34] C. H. Broad would agree with him that justice is only derivatively applied to individual acts, since it is "a special kind of intrinsic good, a property only of very complex states of affairs concerning distribution."[35] For both, justice is to be found only where men are associated together in some form of common life; it is a good of society.

The assertion that justice is entirely dependent on society carries the denial that there is any such thing as a natural right having its basis in man as man. The Social Good theory thus denies that nature or the natural as such provides a basis for justice.

Sidgwick represents all adherents of the theory when he asserts that "no definition that has ever been offered of the Natural exhibits this notion as really capable of furnishing an independent ethical first principle."[36] He claims that natural right provides no standard for man's social relations. The appeal to natural right "presents a problem and not a solution," since it involves finding "in the rights and obligations established by custom in a particular society at a particular time an element that has a binding force beyond what mere custom can give."[37] He allows that "justice is generally, though somewhat vaguely, held to prescribe the fulfillment of all such expectations (of services, etc.) as arise naturally and normally out of the relations voluntary or involuntary, in which we stand towards other human beings."[38] But he claims that this notion of "natural expectation" is not only indefinite, it is "worse than indefinite" in that it conceals a "fundamental conflict of ideas . . . for the word 'natural,' as used in this connection, covers and conceals the whole chasm between the actual and the ideal—what is and what ought to be. . . . The term seems, as ordinarily used, to contain the distinct ideas of (1) the common as opposed to the exceptional, and (2) the original or primitive as contrasted with the result of later conventions and institutions. But it is also used to signify . . . 'what would exist in an

---

[34] *Social Control*, p. 65.
[35] Qu. in Lyons, *Forms and Limits of Utilitarianism*, p. 173.
[36] *Methods of Ethics*, p. 83.
[37] *Ibid.*, pp. 82–83.
[38] *Ibid.*, p. 269.

ideal state of society.' "[39] This confusion, plus the fact that men disagree about the ideal, suffice to show, according to Sidgwick, that the natural provides no criterion for determining what is just.

Mill, too, denies natural right. His essay "Nature" is devoted to refuting the claim that nature in any way constitutes a moral norm for human action. Yet, in his political and social writings, he frequently defends what other writers would call natural rights. His work *On Liberty* analyzes and defends the liberties of individuals and stakes out wide areas of individual choice and determination with which, he claims, society has no right to interfere and to subordinate to social control. In *Representative Government,* he declares expressly that "it is a personal injustice to withhold from any one, unless for the prevention of greater evils, the ordinary privilege of having his voice reckoned in the disposal of affairs in which he has the same interest as other people."[40] Yet he refuses to admit that in all this there is any such thing as a natural right. He declares that he foregoes "any advantage which could be derived to the argument from the idea of abstract right."[41]

Mill's position on liberty is important for understanding the Social Good position as a whole. Its assertion of the conventionality of justice with the consequent denial of natural right does not thereby establish society as an end in itself to which an individual is totally subordinated. Nor does it imply that societies and states cannot be judged in terms of justice. Mill, in fact, would willingly admit that one state is more just than another precisely to the extent that it gives fuller recognition to individual liberties. But as warrant for this claim he would not appeal to natural right. Instead, he holds that such a course of action is more efficient and results in a better society, since each individual is supposed to be the best judge of his own interests.

Individual liberty may be claimed as a requirement of justice by any of the three basic theories. Where they differ lies, not in the claim but in the reason they offer for it. The Social Good position makes it a need of society, or a means for insuring a better society. The Positive Law theory holds that it is an option that has been written into law, while the Natural Right theory maintains that it is a right due to man as man.

[39] *Ibid.,* pp. 272–273.
[40] *Representative Government,* p. 375.
[41] *On Liberty,* p. 97.

SERVING THE SOCIAL GOOD

For the Social Good theory, justice is not coterminous with positive law, nor is it based on natural right. What then is justice, what term is basic to its analysis, how is it best defined? To these questions, the theory answers with the term that best names the whole position: Justice consists in serving and promoting the social good. This is to claim that the good of society is prior to both law and right in the root meaning of justice, and that both of the other notions are in a subordinate position. Law itself is just or unjust according as it serves or fails to serve the good of society. So too, rights belong to man only as he is associated with others in a society.

Since our paradigm authors are the classical Utilitarian philosophers, this position is asserted by the claim that justice is based on utility. Thus, Hume writes that the virtue of justice "derives its existence entirely from its necessary *use* to the intercourse and social state of mankind."[42] Its rules "owe their origin and existence to that utility which results to the public from their strict and regular observance."[43] Although self-interest may have furnished "the original motive to the establishment of justice," he declares that "sympathy with the public interest is the source of the normal approbation which attends the virtue."[44]

Mill holds that "the idea of justice supposes two things: a rule of conduct and a sentiment which sanctions the rules."[45] Like Hume, he traces the moral character, that is its power of commanding an *ought,* to its being a sentiment. But this sentiment he traces to utility—justice, as he says, is "only a particular branch of general utility."[46] If the justice or injustice of an action were "intrinsically peculiar and distinct from all its other qualities," if the feeling itself were *"sui generis* like our sensations of color and taste," then there would be a source and criterion of morality distinct from utility. Mill recognizes that the idea of justice so interpreted constitutes "one of the strongest obstacles to the reception of the Utilitarian doctrine."[47] He

[42] *Enquiry Concerning the Principles of Morals,* p. 186.
[43] *Ibid.,* p. 188.
[44] *A Treatise of Human Nature,* pp. 499–500.
[45] *Utilitarianism,* p. 65.
[46] *Ibid.,* p. 52.
[47] *Ibid.,* p. 51.

is, for this reason, particularly concerned to show that the feeling of justice can be reduced to utility, and is not *sui generis*. Consideration of his argument, however, is better postponed until we come to discuss the obligatoriness of justice.

Sidgwick maintains that both Mill and Hume overemphasize the place of sentiment in their analysis of justice. He also holds that neither appreciates the full complexity of the notion. Considering the various ways in which the term is used, he finds that "justice, exhaustively analyzed, includes several distinct elements combined in a somewhat complex manner."[48] Summarizing his careful and subtle analysis, we obtain the following "elements of justice":

1) Law-observance[49]
2) Equality, whether (a) in the distribution or allotment of rewards and burdens, or (b) impartiality and the avoidance of arbitrary inequality in making and carrying out the law[50]
3) Fulfillment of contract and of natural and normal expectations[51]
4) Reward and punishment according to desert[52]

In claiming that these are elements of justice, Sidgwick does not mean that they are signified or implied in every use of the word "justice." They are rather the senses occurring in different uses, *i.e.*, different ways in which the word may be used. He also is concerned to show that no one of these is sufficient by itself to exhaust the meaning of "justice."

Once he has analyzed the common notion of justice and distinguished its various elements, Sidgwick then proceeds to claim that "utilitarianism furnishes us with a common standard to which the different elements included in the notion of Justice may be reduced."[53] He thinks, however, that the earlier Utilitarians have not done this as well as it might be done. As noted before, they fail to show how really complex the notion of justice is. Hume, he writes, "means by Justice . . . what I should call Order, understood in its widest sense: the observance of the actual system of rules, whether strictly legal or customary, which bind together the different members of any society

48 *Op. cit.*, p. 441.
49 *Ibid.*, p. 265.
50 *Ibid.*, pp. 266–268.
51 *Ibid.*, p. 269.
52 *Ibid.*, p. 279.
53 *Ibid.*, p. 447.

into an organic whole, checking malevolent or otherwise injurious impulses, distributing the different objects of men's clashing desires, and exacting such positive services, customary or contractual, as are commonly recognized as matters of debt."[54] Mill, as we shall see, is said by Sidgwick to fail to account for the obligatory element in justice.

Sidgwick's reduction of the ordinary meaning of justice to utilitarianism can be exhibited in the following series of points:[55]

1) That the habit of Order or Law-observance is conducive to the social happiness is too obvious to need proof.
2) The limits of the duty of Law-observance are to be determined by utilitarian considerations.
3) Impartiality or the negation of arbitrary inequality is a special application of the wider maxim that it cannot be right to treat two persons differently if their cases are similar in all material circumstances. Clearly Utilitarian.
4) Apparent inequality in a certain part of the conduct of individuals is not unjust, for freedom of action is an important source of happiness to the agents and a socially useful stimulus.
5) Claims are recognized as just in that any disappointment of expectations is *pro tanto* an evil, but a greater evil in proportion to the previous security of the expectant individual. Being able to rely on each other's actions is clearly expedient. But there is a vaguer region where we cannot draw a sharp line between valid and invalid claims—injustice shades off into mere hardship.
6) What is desired under the name of Ideal Justice is the distribution of good and evil according to Desert. This is broadly in harmony with Utilitarianism, since we obviously encourage the production of general happiness by rewarding men for felicific conduct.
7) If the good or evil to be distributed have no relation to any conduct on the part of the persons to receive either, or if it is practically impossible to take such considerations into account, then simple Equality is the principle of just apportionment— since it is then the only mode that is not arbitrary.

[54] *Ibid.*, p. 440.
[55] See *ibid.*, pp. 440–446.

Sidgwick ordinarily means by Utilitarianism, or the Utilitarian principle, the greatest happiness of the greatest number. But, as he uses it here to reduce justice to utility, one might well doubt whether utility means anything more than the social good. If it does mean something more, it can only be because this good is understood in a special way as involving more than what is common, general, or social. Yet, in his reduction, it seems that no more than the latter meaning is present, and "utility" means but "social" or "common."

Sidgwick's reduction of the elements of justice to utility understood as the good of society is typical of the Social Good position. All the elements of justice, all its duties and the rules or principles tradition-ally associated with it are held to be based on the social good and to derive their force from that as their source. According to the Natural Right theory, they are not so reducible, since some actions and claims are held to be just in themselves inasmuch as they rest on natural right and are not to be explained by reference to anything else. But this is not so for the Social Good theory. Each element, duty, or rule is just or enters into the makeup of justice only because it is a means to the common utility.

For this reason, the Social Good writers would not accept as adequate the traditional Roman definition of justice as consisting in rendering to each what is his own, his right, or his due. This defini-tion is wrong, Hume writes, because it supposes that right and property exist independent of justice.[56] Property, right, and obliga-tion are all dependent upon justice, and not the other way round, while justice itself, as we have seen, depends on utility.[57]

The theory admits that justice is a matter of rights. Mill even claims that "the essence of the idea of justice is that of a right residing in an individual."[58] The notion of right, however, is not fundamental and prior to that of justice, as it is in Natural Right theory. Thus, Mill goes on to say that "to have a right is to have something which society ought to defend me in the possession of," a claim then we can make upon society. But security is that which is "to everyone's feelings the most vital of all interests" and the ground for "the claim we have on our fellow-creatures to join in making safe for us the very groundwork

[56] See *A Treatise of Human Nature,* p. 526.
[57] See *ibid.,* pp. 490–491.
[58] *Op. cit.,* p. 73.

of our existence."[59] Right, as a claim upon the action or forbearance of others, rests upon the social good. If one asks why society ought to defend him in the possession of his right, Mill answers, "I can give him no other reason than general utility."[60]

To the same effect, thought in different words, Rawls declares that once a practice is recognized as fair or just, as in accord with the common need, "there arises a prima facie duty and a corresponding prima facie right to comply."[61] Blanshard holds that the general good validates a right just as it alone can modify or suspend it. This possibility suffices, he argues, to show that there is no natural right, since such a right must be inalienable and hence belong to men "everywhere and always."[62] For all, the very notion of right supposes dependence on the social good and subordination to it.

Rights are means and contrivances for the good of society, so too is property, which is but one of these rights. Some Social Good authors say nothing at all about property. Yet the position of all is consonant with that of Hume, when he remarks that property is "the creation of society for its interest and happiness."[63]

Sometimes Hume talks as though the creation of property were prior, at least logically, to justice.[64] and he even refers to property as being the object of justice.[65] But by such expressions he does not mean that property is prior to justice as a natural right that antedates the common good of society. For him, property, right, and obligation, all arise together with the notion of justice itself. It is for this reason, as we have seen, that he criticizes those who would explain justice by means of these notions as being "guilty of a very gross fallacy," since it is his contention that "the origin of justice explains that of property: the same artifice gives rise to both."[66]

Equality is judged by some to be so important for the analysis of justice that it is taken as the basic element. The Social Good theory does not deny the importance of equality in the analysis of justice, but it does deny that it is basic. If equality supplies a criterion of justice, it does so because it is itself conducive to the common good of society.

[59] *Ibid.*, p. 67.
[60] *Ibid.*, p. 66.
[61] *The Sense of Justice*, p. 94.
[62] *The Objectivity of Moral Judgment*, pp. 391–392.
[63] *Enquiry Concerning the Principles of Morals*, p. 158.
[64] See *A Treatise of Human Nature*, pp. 490–491.
[65] *Enquiry Concerning the Principles of Morals*, pp. 159–160.
[66] *A Treatise of Human Nature*, p. 491.

Mill, for example, claims that equality of treatment and impartiality can be looked upon as corollary from other principles of justice, inasmuch as they are in part instrumental, "being a necessary condition of the fulfillment of the other obligations of justice."[67] As an example, he says, "if it is a duty to do to each according to his deserts . . . it necessarily follows that we should treat all equally well." But we need not stop here. "This great moral duty," Mill goes on to say, "rests upon a still deeper foundation, being a direct emanation from the first principle of morals, and not a mere logical corollary from secondary or derivative doctrines. It is involved in the very meaning of Utility, or the Greatest Happiness Principle. That principle is a mere form of words without rational signification, unless one person's happiness, supposed equal in degree (with the proper allowance made for kind), is counted for exactly as much as another's. Those conditions being supplied, Bentham's dictum, 'everybody to count for one, nobody for more than one,' might be written under the principle of utility as an explanatory commentary."[68]

The Greatest Happiness Principle is to be understood as a social criterion, *i.e.*, as that of promoting the social good. Mill claims that "society between equals can only exist on the understanding that the interests of all are to be rewarded equally."[69] If, then, Utility means that society and its good must be promoted, and a good society cannot exist without equality, it follows that equal treatment must also be observed. It is, in Mill's metaphor, "a direct emanation from the first principle."

According to Mill, "the clearest and most emphatic form in which the idea of justice is conceived by the general mind . . . involves the notion of desert."[70] As he understands this statement, there is nothing that any adherent to the Social Good theory of justice would deny. The idea of desert, he writes, implies "giving to each what they deserve, that is, good for good as well as evil for evil."[71] both of which are based on their "social utility." The principle of evil for evil provides the ground for the justice of punishment and is analyzed in terms of the sentiment of retribution, which, Mill claims, underlies the sentiment of justice. Of the principle of good for good, Mill claims

[67] *Utilitarianism*, p. 76.
[68] *Ibid.*, p. 77.
[69] *Ibid.*, p. 39.
[70] *Ibid.*, p. 55.
[71] *Ibid.*, pp. 75–76.

that "its social utility is evident" since its denial inflicts a hurt upon society. "He who accepts benefits and denies a return of them when needed, inflicts a real hurt by disappointing one of the most natural and reasonable of expectations and one which he must at least tacitly have encouraged, otherwise the benefits would seldom have been conferred."[72]

Mill does not remark expressly upon the connection of the realization of expectation with utility, perhaps because he thinks it obvious. Society depends upon trust and cooperation and faith in one another, all of which rest on people abiding by what is naturally and normally expected of them. If the disappointment of expectations were everywhere the rule rather than the exception, any sort of cooperation and common life would be immensely difficult, if not impossible. In any case, for Mill, the justification of the principle of desert in the literal sense, as that which makes it just, consists, as we have seen, in its being conducive to the social good, or "social utility," as Mill usually calls it.

This being so, the justice or injustice of inequality is likewise to be decided only in terms of social utility. "Is it just or not that talent or skill should give a title to superior remuneration?" Mill asks. He sketches arguments on both sides and notes that "justice has in this case two sides to it, which it is impossible to bring into harmony." Hence, he concludes, "social utility alone can decide the preference."[73]

THE OBJECTIVITY OF JUSTICE

The social good or utility provides the advocates of the position with an objective norm of justice. The judgment that X is just says something objective about X, namely, that it conforms to the social good. The approbation or approval implicit in the judgment, accordingly, also has an objective basis. It is not merely an expression of subjective emotion on the part of the individual making the statement, as is maintained by the Positive Law theory of all uses of justice meaning anything other than legality.

On the issue regarding the objectivity of justice, the Social Good theory sides with the Natural Right theory against the Positive Law position. Justice, apart from legality, is held to have an objective basis.

[72] *Ibid.*, p. 75.
[73] *Ibid.*, p. 72.

The Social Good authors differ widely, however, concerning the basis of this objectivity, and their differences severely complicate the analysis of the Social Good position on this issue.

The Positive Law position on it is clear and simple: If one says that X is just and means by it more than that X conforms to the law, he says nothing at all about X in itself, but only expresses his subjective, emotional approval of X. The approbative character attributed to X is explained as a feeling of the individual subject making the statement rather than a cognitive judgment about X.

The Social Good position, however, is not this simple. The point at issue is not whether the statement involves more than an expression of feeling but whether or not there is anything objective in it. Some Social Good authors, like Sidgwick, hold that it expresses an objective judgment of reason and, hence, involves more than a feeling. Others, like Hume, however, maintain that the moral approbation involved in a judgment of justice is only a sentiment, but deny that it is subjective and completely dependent on the individual, and affirm instead that it is a sense of what the community objectively feels is good and to be approved.

Thus there are two different ways in which the objectivity of justice can be upheld by the Social Good theory. One bases it on the common feeling of the community regarding what is good. The other bases it on a rational judgment about what is for the social good. Both agree that it has an objective basis independent of the individual's feelings, although both would admit that a statement involving justice, where it means something more than legality, may also indicate the speaker's feeling of approval. The point at issue is whether it indicates anything more than this.

Hume's argument that the moral component of justice is a feeling or sentiment is similar to that advanced by some adherents to the Positive Law theory; in fact, Hume is one of the principal sources for the emotivist theory of moral judgments. The approbation or blame involved in justice "cannot be the work of the judgment," Hume declares, "but of the heart; and is not a speculative proposition or affirmation, but an active feeling or sentiment."[74] It must be a sentiment since it cannot be a reason. To say that an act is just is to have at once a motive and an obligation to act. But reason, according

[74] *Enquiry Concerning the Principles of Morals,* p. 290, Appendix.

to Hume, is incapable of supplying either motivation or obligation; it is "perfectly innert   and can never either prevent or produce any action or affection."[75] Limited solely to discerning and judging either matters of fact or relations of ideas, reason results in the formulation of a proposition that is true or false, and truth or falsity consists "in an agreement or disagreement either to real relations of ideas or to real existence and matters of fact." What is not susceptible of this kind of agreement or disagreement is "incapable of being true or false and can never be an object of reason." But such is the case, Hume claims, of our passions, volitions, and actions. There is no possibility of their agreeing or disagreeing with anything else because they are "original facts and realities," complete in themselves, without any reference to other passions, volitions, and actions. " 'Tis impossible," Hume concludes, "they can be pronounced either true or false, and be either contrary or conformable to reason." Since justice, like a passion or a volition, provides a motive for action, and since it results in an *ought*, it cannot be based on reason that provides no motive and is concerned solely with what *is*.

Up to this point, there is nothing with which an emotivist adherent to the Positive Law theory necesarily would disagree. Yet Hume is no proponent of that position. Justice may rest on a feeling, but this of itself does not make a judgment of justice subjective and entirely relative to the individual. The feeling upon which justice is based is, according to Hume, a social and public feeling that arises in any man's breast when he is confronted with circumstances in which the social good is involved. Hume allows, as we have seen, that concern for the public utility may be in the first place purely a matter of self-interest. Living in association with others, pursuing common ends, provides relief for the weakness of the individual and the poverty of nature; then, too, his need for others also is reinforced by a natural sympathy for his fellowman. "Self-interest is the original motive to the establishment of justice," Hume writes, "but a sympathy with public interest is the source of the moral approbation which attends that virtue."[76]

This feeling for the public good and its rules is not a private and accidental or arbitrary occurrence. It is "inviolably established in the nature of man and of the world in which he lives," Hume says.[77]

[75] *A Treatise of Human Nature*, p. 458.
[76] *Ibid.*, pp. 499–500.
[77] *Enquiry Concerning the Principles of Morals*, pp. 4, 171.

"The intercourse of sentiments in society and conversation makes us form some general unalterable standard by which we may approve or disapprove of characters and manners."[78] Hume even speaks of a "natural standard," although by this he means no more than that it arises regularly among men living in society;[79] justice is still an artificial virtue in the sense discussed above. "The convenience and necessity for justice is so universal and everywhere points to the same rules that the habit takes place in all societies," Hume writes.[80] For this reason, he claims that "the rules of justice are not arbitrary."[81] The same reason serves also to show that a judgment based on those rules is not subjective. It rests on the general feeling of the society regarding what should or should not be approved.

The feeling, it should be pointed out, concerns only the approbation or censure entering into a moral judgment. Besides that, and prior to it, there is a judgment regarding the utility of the action or object being judged, and this, for Hume, is a work of reason. A judgment regarding the justice of an act thus involves two distinct elements for him. First, one has to determine whether the quality or action is useful or not; this is a matter of fact and, hence, a work of reason. Second, one has to approve the useful and prefer it to the pernicious; and only this is for Hume a sentiment based on what men socially have come to feel should be approved.[82]

Mill agrees with Hume that justice contains two distinct elements. Although he describes them differently, they reduce to much the same. Justice consists, he writes, in "a rule of conduct and a sentiment which sanctions the rule."[83] The rule of conduct concerns men's social actions, which, as we have seen above in discussing the dependence of justice upon society, are to be governed by social utility. The sanction of this rule refers to the specifically moral and approbative character attaching to it, and, in identifying it expressly with a sentiment, Mill agrees with Hume regarding the source or basis of morality. He differs somewhat from him in placing more weight upon the feeling for retaliation, which, he claims, underlies the sentiment of justice. But he asserts even more strongly that the acceptance or

[78] *Ibid.*, p. 229.
[79] See *ibid.*, p. 214.
[80] *Ibid.*, p. 203.
[81] *A Treatise of Human Nature*, p. 484.
[82] *Enquiry Concerning the Principles of Morals*, p. 235.
[83] *Op. cit.*, p. 65.

rejection of a moral rule does not depend on blind impulse or arbitrary choice, but falls within the cognizance of reason, particularly regarding the determination of its consequences. Thus, on both counts, that is, as involving reason to determine the social utility and as a sentiment that is social, a judgment of justice has an objective basis.

Sidgwick agrees with both Mill and Hume regarding the objectivity of justice, but he differs from them about its basis. It is more than merely a social feeling or a sentiment approving what is for the good of all. It also involves a cognitive judgment, the work of what Sidgwick calls the Practical Reason. He is as emphatic as Hume in asserting that no *ought*-statement can be derived from any number of *is*-statements. But, unlike him, he does not maintain that the determination of the moral *ought* is completely divorced from reason. A moral judgment is a rational judgment, but it is a work of practical reason regarding what is to be done and not of speculative reason about what is the case.

In common with Hume and Mill, Sidgwick would hold that the statement that X is just contains at least two elements: (1) that X is for the social good, and (2) that what is for the social good ought to be done. The first of these, all three agree, concerns the determination of a matter of fact for which deliberation and reason are needed. But whereas Hume and Mill regard the second as a feeling, Sidgwick holds that this too is a work of reason and knowledge. The moral faculty by which we are aware of what ought to be done cannot be a sense, he argues, since, otherwise, two people could differ completely about it without either ever being in error. Our moral judgments are more than feelings, he maintains, because they are intrinsically universal and one is "unreasonable not to do" their bidding.[84] They rest on an intuition, not a reasoning from fact or principle, but a seeing that such-and-such is so: "the power of seeing clearly that certain kinds of actions are right and reasonable in themselves, apart from their consequences."[85]

The nature and content of this moral intuition is more appropriately discussed below when we come to consideration of the obligatoriness of justice. But that, for Sidgwick, a moral judgment is based upon an intuition, or a seeing that something is the case, is sufficient to show that he affirms the objectivity of justice. That what is just

[84] *Methods of Ethics,* p. 34; cf. p. 77.
[85] *Ibid.,* p. 200.

enjoys the approval of men is accordingly something more than merely a subjective feeling in those having it.

THE OBLIGATORINESS OF JUSTICE

The norm of justice is a moral rule declaring what ought to be done. If now we ask why one ought to be just, the question for the Social Good position reduces to asking, why one ought to do what conforms to the social good: Why should one do what is socially useful? Of course, if one does not, one becomes subject to the sanctions of society. Then, too, one's action or failure to act may frustrate and thwart the achievement of a valuable objective. Both of these supply reasons or grounds for acting for the common good. Neither one, nor the two together, suffices, however, to explain the obligation of justice as it is understood by the Social Good theory. But the effort to explain why they do not poses a special difficulty for the theory. On the one hand, it wants to maintain that the obligation of justice is moral and categorical: One ought to do what is just since it is just. On the other hand, it also wants to root this obligation in the social good and so tends to reduce it to a pragmatic and hypothetical *ought:* One ought to do what is just in order to bring about the social good. This tension within the Social Good theory is seen most clearly in Mill's account of obligation and Sidgwick's criticism and revision of it.

The rule of justice differs from other moral rules, Mill declares, only in the fact that the requirements that it lays down, "regarded collectively, stand higher in the scale of social utility, and are therefore of more paramount obligation than any others."[86] Since they "concern the essentials of human well-being more nearly," they are "of more absolute obligation than any other rules for the guidance of life.[87] Mill considers in some detail several of the traditional maxims of justice, such as those "which forbid mankind to hurt one another . . . avoiding wrongfully withholding from him something which is his due . . . giving to each what they deserve," together with the "judicial virtues" of impartiality and equality which, he claims, are "instrumental to carrying into effect" those just cited.[88] All these

[86] *Op. cit.*, p. 79.
[87] *Ibid.*, p. 73.
[88] *Ibid.*, pp. 74–76.

rules, according to Mill, suppose and depend upon the primacy of social utility, and we saw above how he would accomplish this reduction in the case of the principle of equality.

We have also seen that for Mill the sanction of justice derives from the sentiment that accompanies the rule of conduct. He distinguishes between external and internal sanctions. Among the first, he enumerates "the hope of favour and fear of displeasure from our fellow-creatures or from the Ruler of the Universe, along with whatever we may have of sympathy or affection for them, or of love and awe of him."[89] He identifies the internal sanction with duty or conscience, which is a "subjective feeling in our own minds." Applied to justice, this would be the feeling that we ought to do what is just and ought to refrain from doing what is unjust; that it is good to do what is just and bad to do what is unjust—right in the one case and wrong in the other. It involves a feeling of moral obligation, which, according to Mill, "consists in the existence of a mass of feelings which must be broken though in order to do what violates our standard of right, and which, if we do nevertheless violate that standard will probably have to be encountered afterwards in the form of remorse."[90]

The idea of penal sanction and constraint is central to Mill's understanding of this sentiment. "When we think that a person is bound in justice to do a thing, it is an ordinary form of language to say that he ought to be compelled to do it." So, too, we feel that acts of injustice should be punished, and the punishment "would always give us pleasure and chime in with our feelings of fitness."[91]

This appeal to fitness is significant, since it implies that the use of constraint and punishment may be either fit or unfit, or, in other words, right or not right. In fact, for Mill, the feeling of *ought* involved in justice includes the feeling that one may be *rightfully* compelled to do it.[92] Thus, insofar as the sanction of justice refers to constraint and compulsion, it is qualified by the further feature that it must be exercised rightfully.

Mill notes that a person involved in an issue of justice may claim a certain performance as a matter of right and, on nonperformance, is entitled to complain that he has suffered injury. Thus, in justice,

[89] *Ibid.*, p. 33.
[90] *Ibid.*, pp. 34–35.
[91] *Ibid.*, p. 59.
[92] See *ibid.*, p. 61.

there is "a right in some person, correlative to the moral obligation" in another.

Thus, for Mill, and for the Social Good proponents generally, the use of constraint and penal sanction must itself be justified by right. Consequently, if men ought to do justice, it is not only because they will be punished if they do not. They will have violated a right, which is something that they *ought* not do. But right, as we have seen, rests on more than law and its sanctions. This much suffices to distinguish the Social Good position on obligation from that of the Positive Law theory. It is also significantly different from that of the Natural Right theory.

Mill claims, as we saw above (p. 91) that justice is a complex of two sentiments—"the impulse of self-defence and the feeling of sympathy." But what makes the justice more than natural and instinctive, what makes it moral, is the fact that these feelings are completely subordinated to the good of society at large. Justice may in origin owe "its peculiar impressiveness and energy of self-assertion" to the impulse for self-defense and retaliation, but the thirst for retaliation "derives its intensity, as well as its moral justification, from the extraordinarily important and impressive kind of utility which is concerned"—the utility of society regarding its most important needs and purposes.[93]

Such is Mill's claim. Yet the question can be raised whether he does not still have only a pragmatic and hypothetical *ought*. Issues of social utility involve interests of great importance, and to preserve and promote those interests one ought to work for the social good. But why ought one preserve and promote those interests? Would it be wrong not to? Mill appears to think so, but he supplies no further reason. It may be true that if one wants the good of society he ought to be just. But there is nothing peculiarly moral about such an *ought* as this. Furthermore, to claim that it is would involve one in trying to deduce a moral *ought* statement from premises that contain no such *ought*, or what has come to be known, on one interpretation, as the naturalist fallacy.

The Social Good authors are peculiarly sensitive to this danger. Hume, in a famous passage, warns expressly against it. After noting that moralists frequently move from a series of propositions expressed entirely with *is* or *is not* to injunctions formed with *ought* and *ought*

[93] *Ibid.,* p. 66.

not, he remarks that "this change is imperceptible, but is, however, of the last consequence. For as this *ought* or *ought not* expresses some new relation or affirmation, 'tis necessary that it should be observed and explained; and at the same time that a reason should be given, for what seems altogether inconceivable, how this new relation can be a deduction from the others, which are entirely different from it."[94]

Sidgwick, too, observes, much to the same effect, that Bentham sometimes writes as though the word "right" means nothing but "conducive to the general happiness," but then he warns that Bentham cannot be understood to really mean this; "for the proposition that it is conducive to general happiness to take general happiness as an end of action, though not exactly a tautology, can hardly serve as the fundamental principle of a moral system."[95] Further, it was this passage of Sidgwick's that seems to have led G. E. Moore to reflections that resulted in his analysis of the naturalist fallacy.[96]

Mill's analysis of obligation comes close to making the same claim that Sidgwick criticizes in Bentham. In fact, he does not hesitate to speak of indispensability becoming a moral necessity, and, thus, appears to pass from a hypothetical to a categorical obligation. "Our notion of the claim we have on our fellow-creatures to join in making safe for us the very groundwork of our existence gathers feelings around it so much more intense than those concerned in any of the more common cases of utility that the differences in degree (as is often the case in psychology) becomes a real difference in kind. . . . The feelings are so powerful, and we count so positively on finding a responsive feeling in others (all being alike interested), that *ought* and *should* grow into *must,* and recognized indispensability becomes a moral necessity, analogous to physical, and often not inferior to it in binding force."[97]

Sidgwick is not convinced by this account and criticizes Mill for not adequately explaining the distinctly moral feature of obligation. He distinguishes four senses or ways in which the expression "X ought to be done" can be understood: (1) It may mean that X is "the fittest or only fit means to the realization of some end understood if not expressly stated."[98] This is a teleological *ought,* since the judgment

94 *A Treatise of Human Nature,* p. 469.
95 *Op. cit.,* p. 26, Note 1.
96 See Prior, *Logic and the Basis of Ethics,* p. 105.
97 *Op. cit.,* p. 67.
98 *Methods of Ethics,* p. 26.

involved has the form: If you want Y, then X ought to be done, or X
is a means to Y. (2) Again, the expression may "affirm no more than
the existence of a specific emotion in the mind of the person who
utters it . . . a feeling of approbation or satisfaction" or the claim
that "this subjective fact of my approbation is all that there is any
ground on reflection to affirm";[99] this is the approbative *ought,* since
the reason I have for affirming that X ought to be done in this case is
my approval of X. (3) Again, when we say that a person ought to do
X, we may "mean that he is bound under penalties to do it—the
particular penalty considered being the pain that will accrue to him
directly or indirectly from the dislike of his fellow-creatures" or the
penalties of human or divine law;[100] this is the punitive *ought.* (4)
Finally, we have what for Sidgwick is the distinctively moral *ought*
when, in judging that X ought to be done, we give expression to a
notion that is "too elementary to admit of any formal definition"
although it implies that X is thought to be capable of being brought
about voluntarily or, at least, of serving as an ideal or pattern to
follow, and that the judgment that it ought to be done "gives an
impulse or motive to action" which it would be unreasonable not to
follow.[101]

Sidgwick would not deny that a moral judgment that X is just and
ought to be done may involve all the other types of *ought.* But he does
claim that to be moral it must include the last distinctively moral
ought, and he finds it a shortcoming in Hume and Mill that they have
endeavored to do without such an *ought.* Hume attempts to reduce
the obligatoriness of justice to an approbative *ought,* social rather than
merely individual in character, but still approbative. Mill would
account for it by combining a teleological and a punitive *ought.*
Neither, according to Sidgwick, has succeeded in accounting for what
is distinctively moral in the obligatoriness of justice, since they have
overlooked the fundamental intuition of the moral *ought.* "The utilitarian method," he writes, "could not be made coherent and harmoni-
ous without this fundamental intuition."[102] Knowing that X is for
the common good does not of itself impose the duty of doing X. For
this, Sidgwick would maintain, we must also know that the common

99 *Ibid.,* pp. 26–27.
100 *Ibid.,* pp. 29, 31.
101 *Ibid.,* pp. 32–37.
102 *Ibid.,* pp. xvi–xvii.

good ought to be done. But knowing that a certain course of action is just as conforming to the social good, we then also see that it ought to be done—and the *ought* in this case is distinctively moral.

Sidgwick's position on this matter of moral intuition is summed up shortly in the statement that "there are certain absolute practical principles, the truth of which, when they are explicitly stated, is manifest; but they are of too abstract a nature, and too universal in their scope, to enable us to ascertain by immediate application of them what we ought to do in any particular case; particular duties have still to be determined by some other method,"[103] namely, by finding out what in the concrete is for the greater good, which, on his understanding of it, is the method of Utilitarianism.

Among the immediately evident moral intuitions, Sidgwick enumerates the following:

(1) If a kind of conduct that is right (or wrong) for me is not right (or wrong) for some one else, it must be on the ground of some difference between the two cases, other than the fact that I and he are different persons.

(2) A corresponding proposition stated in respect of what ought to be done *to*—not *by*—different individuals.

These two together constitute the Golden Rule, which, as stated precisely, amounts to this: 'It cannot be right for *A* to treat *B* in a manner in which it would be wrong for *B* to treat *A*, merely on the ground that they are two different individuals, and without there being any difference between the natures or circumstances of the two which can be stated as a reasonable ground for difference of treatment.'

(3) That general rules of law should be applied impartially is another application of it.

(4) A smaller present good is not to be preferred to a greater future good.

(5) The good of any one individual is of no more importance from the point of view . . . of the Universe, than the good of any

---

[103] *Ibid.*, p. 379.

other; unless there are special grounds for believing that more good is likely to be realized in the one case than in the other.

(6) From these two, the Maxim of Benevolence: Each one is morally bound to regard the good of any other individual as much as his own, except insofar as he judges it to be less, when impartially viewed, or less certainly knowable or attainable by him.[104]

These principles, Sidgwick claims, are "genuine intuitions of the Practical Reason." He regards "the apprehension, with more or less distinctness, of these abstract truths, as the permanent basis of the common conviction that the fundamental precepts of morality are essentially reasonable."[105]

In his account of moral obligation, Sidgwick comes closest to the position of the Natural Right theory, and, as we have had occasion to note before, the question arises whether he should or should not be counted as a proponent of the Social Good theory of justice. But while his position of a fundamental moral intuition may be a feature he shares with the naturalists, this claim does not by itself remove him from the adherents to the Social Good position. What is essential to this position, here as in regard to the other issues, is whether reference to the social good is needed in every case to account for the obligation of justice. On this point, Sidgwick joins company with both Hume and Mill in common opposition to the Natural Right position.

For all three, justice imposes a serious and distinct moral obligation. What is just ought to be done and not merely because failure to do so will bring down the sanctions of law and of society. The obligation of justice is a duty men owe to society, resting on their responsibility for the social good.

JUSTICE AND BENEVOLENCE

The Social Good theory agrees with the Natural Right theory in maintaining that justice is not to be identified with obedience to the law. This follows, of course, from the refusal to identify justice with conformity to law. Thus, after giving the reasons why he refuses to make this identification, which have been cited above (p. 83), Sidg-

104 *Ibid.*, pp. 379–382.
105 *Ibid.*, pp. 383–384.

wick says explicitly: "We must then distinguish justice from what has been called the virtue or duty of order, or law-observance,"[106] and this statement is representative of all proponents of the Social Good theory of justice.

The Social Good authors would not disagree with the naturalists that justice can be described as the virtue of rendering to each his due. They would say only that this formulation is itself derivative from another that is more basic, since what is due and a matter of right is itself just only because it promotes the common good. Accordingly, on this theory, there is another and better definition of justice as a virtue: It is the virtue of acting for the social good.

This characterization of justice as a virtue follows, of course, from the position already taken concerning the nature of justice. Yet there are special problems in the Social Good account of justice as a virtue that distinguish it from the other theories. In particular, the relation of justice to benevolence, on the one hand, and to expediency, on the other, raise such difficulties as to lead to considerable discussion.

The theory holds that justice is a distinct virtue. But it must be said at once that there is a strong tendency within the theory to assimilate it to benevolence. Generally, the adherents of the theory endeavor to overcome this tendency, although in the case of Bentham even the attempt to distinguish is lacking, and justice is identified as "nothing more than a part of the dictates of benevolence."[107] But, in this, he is exceptional, as we can see once we consider our paradigm authors.

The difficulty of distinguishing justice from benevolence arises from the fact that for the theory both have the same source and the same end. Both are rooted in the instinct or feeling of sympathy that we have for our fellowman, what Hume calls our "natural philanthropy," and both aim at the good of others as a common good. How then do they differ? The Social Good authors give different answers.

Hume finds the difference, as we have already seen, in the fact that benevolence is a "natural virtue," whereas justice is "artificial," as supposing reason, forethought, design, social union.[108] Benevolence, he writes, "applies directly by instinct to simple, particular objects," whereas justice supposes a "whole scheme or system concurred in by

---

[106] *Ibid.*, p. 265.
[107] Ogden, *Bentham's Theory of Fictions*, p. 125, Note 2.
[108] *Enquiry Concerning the Principles of Morals*, p. 258.

the whole or majority of society."[109] Virtue, for Hume, is much like an emotion, in being a feeling or sentiment that arises in us when we confront a certain quality, object, or action. Benevolence, arising from our sympathy with others, may be exercised whenever and wherever we wish to help another. Justice, on the contrary, may demand of us actions that we do not want to perform, and that we even find displeasing. In a particular case, justice may act "contrary to public interest"[110] and contrary even to our sense of humanity, as when "judges take from a poor man to give to a rich . . . bestow on the dissolute the labor of the industrious; and put into the hands of the vicious the means of harming both themselves and others."[111] The justification of such actions, their justice, lies only in their being advantageous to society in the long run, once all things are taken into account.

Mill places the difference between the two virtues in a feature implicit in Hume's account: in the fact that the services dictated by justice can be claimed as a right by their recipient, whereas beneficence, as he calls it, is essentially unconstrained. He says that it corresponds to the difference between what some ethical writers denote by "the ill-chosen expressions, duties of perfect and of imperfect obligation; the latter being those in which though the act is obligatory, the particular occasions of performing it are left to our choice; as in the case of charity or beneficence, which we are indeed bound to practise, but not towards any definite person, nor at any prescribed time. . . . Duties of perfect obligation are those duties in virtue of which a correlative right resides in some persons or persons." It is the existence of such a right, Mill go on to say, that constitutes "the specific difference between justice and generosity or beneficence."[112]

Sidgwick analyzes the difference between the two virtues by considering that part of conduct beyond the sphere of law where questions of justice arise. From such a consideration, he claims that "we may observe that the notion of justice always involves allotment of something considered as advantageous or disadvantageous: whether it be money or other material means of happiness, or praise, or affection,

---

[109] *Ibid.*, p. 303; see also *A Treatise of Human Nature*, p. 579.
[110] *A Treatise of Human Nature*, p. 497.
[111] *Ibid.*, p. 579.
[112] *Utilitarianism*, p. 61.

or other immaterial good, or some merited pain or loss."[113] Justice is thus said to differ from benevolence in the fact that it raises questions of the right allotment. It would seem that, in Hume's language, this would count as a feature showing that justice is "artificial."

But whether artificial or involving a right, or an allotment, justice, for all of these writers, ultimately consists in serving and promoting the social good. The just, in other words, consists in what is useful for society. But then the question arises whether justice, on this view of it, is not reduced to expediency, and, if so, how it is a virtue at all. Thus, we come to the second of the two problems that arise with special urgency within the theory, although Mill is the only author to consider it at any length.

Mill notes that in practice the just is often opposed to the expedient, and although he himself admits that they are not the same, he emphasizes that the difference between them is not one of opposition. When he refers to expediency, as when he refers to utility, Mill usually understands social expediency or social utility. He rules out that which promotes a merely individual good. But, among the social goods, some are more weighty and of greater consequence than others; they "concern the essentials of human well-being more nearly, and are therefore of more absolute obligation, than any other rules for the guidance of life."[114] The rules he is referring to are those already considered above, such "primary moralities" as not to hurt another, to render to each his due, and to treat all equally absolutely or proportionately. Justice, for Mill, differs from expediency or policy in dealing with such matters as these.

According to Mill, "All cases of justice are also cases of expediency," but not the converse. Not all cases of expediency are cases of justice, since they lack the "peculiar sentiment," consisting of the "natural feeling of resentment, moralized by being made coextensive with the demands of social good."[115] This is only to say again that justice is concerned with more important matters, so that its claim "assumes that character of absoluteness, that apparent infinity, and incommensurability with all other considerations, which constitute the distinction between the feeling of right and wrong and that of

[113] *Methods of Ethics*, p. 268.
[114] *Op. cit.*, p. 73.
[115] *Ibid.*, pp. 79–80.

ordinary expediency and inexpediency."[116] Thus, justice, for Mill, is only the most serious expediency about the most important matters.

Sidgwick would not have to accept this conclusion of Mill's, since he admits a "fundamental moral intuition," and its presence would always serve to distinguish justice from expedience. An issue of justice would impose a moral obligation lacking from cases of expediency, where the only *ought* involved would be hypothetical as concerning the best means to achieve an end. Yet, in taking such a position, Sidgwick is exceptional among the Social Good authors and approaches again, as noted before, to the Naturalist position. Mill's account is more typical of the Social Good position as such.

With this we have seen the position of the Social Good theory on all six of the fundamental issues regarding justice. The construction of the theory is complete. We conclude by summarizing the propositions that serve to identify the Social Good theory of justice.

(1) Justice and injustice are not exclusively dependent on positive law.

> Justice is applicable in areas, such as private life, where law does not and should not apply.

> Justice exists even where there is no organized positive law.

(2) Justice provides a criterion for the goodness of law.

> Law may be just or unjust.

> Law and government both presuppose justice.

(3) Justice derives exclusively from society and consists ultimately in promoting the social good.

> Justice is entirely dependent on society and not on the nature of man as such.

> Justice is not based on natural right.

> Justice is not adequately defined as rendering to each his due.

> All rights and all duties of justice are based upon the social good and subservient to it.

> All questions of justice must ultimately be decided in terms of the social good.

[116] *Ibid.,* p. 67.

(4) Justice is an objective norm for human actions.

    The social good provides an objective criterion of what ought to be done.

    The approbation of justice has an objective basis and is not merely an individual's subjective feeling.

(5) Justice imposes a moral duty based on the social good and not merely on legal sanctions.

(6) Justice is a distinct virtue, disposing one to act for the social good.

    Although not to be confused with it, justice is similar to benevolence.

6

The Natural Right Theory
of Justice

THE position of the Natural Right theory on the six fundamental issues regarding justice is summed up in the following propositions:

(1) Justice and injustice are not exclusively dependent on positive law.

(2) Justice provides a criterion for the goodness of law.

(3) Justice is based on natural right and consists in rendering to each his due.

(4) Justice is an objective norm for human actions.

(5) Justice is obligatory in itself, apart from social and legal sanctions.

(6) Justice, as a virtue, is distinct from all other virtues.

Stated in this summary fashion, the position of the Natural Right theory seems to be very similar to that taken by the Social Good theory. On five of the six issues they take the same position and disagree only on the third. Whereas the one bases justice on the social good, the other maintains that it rests fundamentally on natural right.

This difference, however, is crucial and affects the position taken on all the other issues. For the one theory, it is natural right that provides the ultimate criterion of law, that furnishes an objective norm for human action, and that makes the observance of justice obligatory as such. The Social Good theory denies the very existence of natural right and hence provides a different basis for justice as a criterion of law and as an objective and obligatory norm for action. Although the two theories take the same position on each of these issues, they do so for different reasons. They give fundamentally different accounts of justice. Hence, the two theories are by no means as close to each other as at first appears.

The Natural Right theory is the most complex of the basic theories of justice. More variation is found among its proponents than among those of the other theories. There are more subclasses or species falling under the generic position. This fact makes the theory the most difficult one to expound and describe. We need to cut through the welter of differences and disagreements to reach the minimum on which all agree. This, of course, has been our purpose in constructing the other basic positions in the two preceding chapters. But, in this case, it is well at the start to state the minimum that serves to identify one as an adherent to the Natural Right position. To do so will serve to indicate how the word "natural" is to be understood in the name of the position.

There are two negative notes and one positive note that serve to identify the position. The theory denies, first, that justice is identical with legality, and, second, that the interest or good of society provides its basic meaning. Third, it asserts that justice is based on the nature of man. In other words, it holds that justice answers to something more than the needs of law and of society. Justice answers also to the need of man as man. It is held, furthermore, that this need underlies the relation of justice to law and to society.

To repeat, all that is required to establish a writer as a proponent of the Natural Right position is the denial that justice is exclusively a matter of law and of the social good, conjoined with the assertion that both of these must serve the interests of man. Justice is held to be primarily and basically a human good, and only secondarily and derivatively a legal or a social good.

Most, but not all, of the proponents of the Natural Right theory also assert the existence of natural law. Some, as we shall see, even define justice in terms of law, by which they mean ultimately the natural law. It might thus appear that natural law provides the identifying note of this position on justice that I call the Natural Right theory.

Such is not the case, however. As noted in the preliminary description of the basic theories of justice in Chapter 2 (pp. 25 ff.), it would cause endless and needless confusion to have two opposed theories both holding that justice is based on law, but differing about the basic law. The controversy over justice is not free of this confusion, but there is no need to repeat the confusion in the analysis of the controversy. But, what is more important for our purposes, the Natural Right position does not always in fact involve an assertion of natural law. While there are Natural Right authors who affirm their belief in natural law, there are also others who subscribe to the Natural Right position as we describe it, but deny the existence of natural law.

To cite but one example, Julius Stone maintains that there are certain "quasi-absolutes of justice," but denies that they belong to or derive from any natural law.[1] But, when he comes to express these "absolutes," he declares that the basic one is the precept that "social arrangements should as a minimum (even if only as a minimum) respect every man's claim to perform, entertain, and articulate his own interests."[2] Holding then that every man has a right to such a claim, and a claim to which he can appeal against society and its laws, Stone thereby shows that he is a proponent of the Natural Right theory of justice.

With these cautionary remarks by way of qualifying the limited sense in which the identifying term is to be understood, we can now list the main adherents or proponents of the theory.

The same qualifications made about categorizing the Positive Law and the Social Good authors apply to the above list. In fact, they apply most strongly here, since there is much less similarity among the Natural Right authors than among those of the other two theories. The Natural Right position is a dialectical construction, and a writer is to be counted as a proponent of it if his theory of justice approaches it as a limit. It is maintained that the authors listed above would assert all six of the identifying propositions with which we began. They

[1] See *Human Law and Human Justice,* pp. 340–341.
[2] *Ibid.,* p. 333.

Proponents of the Natural Right Theory

Aquinas	Maritain
Aristotle	Messner
Augustine	Montesquieu
Blackstone	Paine
Brentano	Plato*
Brown	Pufendorf
Brunner	Ritchie
Burke	Rommen
Burlamaqui	D. Ross
Bynkershoek	Ryan
Cicero	St. Germain
Frankena	Scheler
Green	Simon
Grotius	Stammler*
Hart	Suarez
Hooker	Taparelli
Hegel*	Del Vecchio
Jefferson	Vitoria
Kant*	Whewell
Leibniz	Wilson
Locke	Wolff

* One of the dialectically difficult authors and, hence, especially subject to the qualifications of classification noted above, p. 22.

would do so for different reasons, since, for many of them, the theory of justice is but a small part of a much larger philosophical enterprise. This is notably true of Kant and Hegel. Our concern, however, is the theory of justice, and we are only remotely interested with what might be called the systematic interests of a philosopher in fitting an account of justice into a larger philosophical system. Authors as different as Aristotle, Augustine, Kant, and Scheler can take one and the same position about justice even though their teachings diverge in many other respects.

Because of the diversity among its proponents, it is hard to find paradigm authors of the Natural Right position. It becomes necessary to refer to more authors than were used in constructing the other two theories, since, to determine accurately the position of the theory, it is necessary to describe at least the main variants of it. The main split occurs between what might be called the individualistic and the nonindividualistic versions of the theory. One bases natural right ultimately on the nature of man as an individual and finds it useful to conceive of man existing apart from any organized political society. The other version bases natural right on the social nature of man and makes no appeal to man existing as an individual in a state of nature apart from society. The paradigm authors of these two versions of the Natural Right theory are, respectively, Locke and Maritain.

Still other variants need to be taken into account. Both Locke and Maritain talk explicitly of the natural rights of individuals as well as of natural law, although they differ widely about the latter. Yet there are also proponents of the Natural Right theory who may have little to say about either the natural rights of individuals or about natural law. Aristotle, for instance, develops his theory of justice almost entirely around the notion of equality, and he says nothing at all about natural law. Aquinas, on the other hand, has much to say about natural law, but very little about the natural rights of individuals. But, by taking all four writers as the paradigm authors of the Natural Right theory, we can indicate the variation possible within it and something of the range of discussion to be found among the proponents of the theory.

It may seem strange to take three philosophers belonging to one main philosophical tradition as paradigm for a position that is shared in common by different philosophies. But I do so for the same reason that I took the Utilitarian philosophers as paradigm for the Social Good position. Both groups come closer than any others to stating all of the central identifying propositions of the position as a whole. They are, as it were, more central to the common position than other writers. They come closer to reaching the limit position that I am attempting to delineate. Yet it is important to emphasize that the generic position that I am calling the Natural Right theory of justice is not the property of any one philosopher or philosophical school. It is a common position that many writers, non-Aristotelian as well as Aristotelian, approximate. It is a dialectical construction, and not any one philosopher's theory of justice.

Rendering Each His Right or Due

There is no doubt that the most famous and influential definition in the entire discussion of justice is the one the Roman lawyers enshrined in the Justinian Code: "Justice is the constant and perpetual will of rendering to each his right"—*Justitia est constans et perpetua voluntas jus suum cuique tribuens.*[3] The definition is even older than the code. It is found in Cicero, although without the word *"jus,"* so that the last part might better be translated as rendering to each *his own.*[4] It also appears in the beginning of Plato's *Republic,* where it is attributed to the Greek poet Simonides: *to ta opheilomena hekasto apodidonai dikaion,* although the word *opheilomena* is better understood as *what is due* or *fitting* rather than right or one's own.[5]

This is not the first time that we have met this definition. There is good reason for maintaining, however, that it can be claimed most appropriately by the Natural Right position. Both the Social Good theory and the Positive Law theory would accept it only on the understanding that what is one's own or due or right is the work of society or of positive law. The notion itself is not for these theories primitive for the analysis of justice, as it is for the Natural Right position.

Aquinas is representative of the position in his acceptance and defense of the adequacy of the Justinian definition. It is true that he qualifies his acceptance of it with the statement that "it must be understood rightly," and this much could be claimed by adherents of the other positions. Unlike the latter, however, Aquinas explicitly affirms that "rendering each his right states the proper object and matter of justice."[6] His qualifications apply only to the way the formulation must be understood to indicate the full definition of justice as a virtue; in other words, his qualifications are more concerned with the theory of virtue than of justice. Put in its "proper form," the definition would read, he says, as follows: "Justice is the habit by which one, from a constant and perpetual will, renders to each his right." There is no question whatever but that "right" is the key term for the analysis of justice.

Although Aristotle has much to say about justice, he does not actually cite this definition. Yet he would accept it, since, as we will see later, he holds that there are things that are naturally just that a man may claim as his right or his own.

Locke does not elaborate a theory of justice by and for itself, and what he thinks about the nature of justice has to be gathered mainly

[3] *Digest* I. 1, *De justitia et jure,* 10.
[4] *De finibus,* 5, 23.
[5] *The Republic,* 331e.
[6] *Summa Theologica,* 2–2, 58, 1.

from what he has to say about society and government. That he would accept the classical definition, even though he does not explicitly use it, is evident from the way he refers to justice. He holds that "where there is no property there is no injustice," but by "property" he understands "a right to anything," so that injustice is "the invasion or violation of that right."[7] Hence, justice consists in the observance of one's right, the basis of which is constituted for Locke, as we shall see, by natural right.

Maritain declares expressly that "the notion of justice is enveloped in that of right, but it is there in an implicit state, and it is by means of the very notion of right that it is disengaged and brought to light. Justice is defined by means of right as rendering to each *his due*."[8]

Maritain appeals here to the notion of due as well as of right, and it is time to see how these terms are related. As is already evident, there are three different ways of formulating the essential part of the classical definition according as one uses the notion of *right*, of *due*, or of *one's own*. What reason is there, if any, for holding that three formulations are equivalent? And, if so, what is gained by way of emphasis in using one of the terms in preference to either of the others? In answering these questions, which will take us closer to the heart of the Natural Right position, Maritain is more explicit than the other paradigm authors.

Of these three terms, the most ambiguous is "right." Indeed, it has the same basic ambiguity as "just." It has a general use in which it can be applied to any action that is judged to be morally good; it can apply to any virtue. Thus, it can be said of a man that he did *right* in stopping his drinking before he got drunk, or that it is *right* to be temperate. Corresponding to this adjectival use—"such-and-such being the *right* thing to do"—there is the substantival use in, "I have the right to do so," when it means, as Maritain writes, "only that in acting so I would do nothing wrong or prohibited by law."[9] "Right," in either this adjectival or substantival use, has as its opposite the word "wrong." In this general sense of "right," there is nothing peculiar to justice, and it is mentioned here only to distinguish it from a more particular use of the term proper to justice.

This particular use appears when we say that we have a right to

---

[7] *An Essay Concerning Human Understanding*, IV, iii, 18.
[8] *Neuf Leçons sur les notions premieres de la philosophie morale*, p. 167.
[9] *Ibid.*, p. 163.

such things as life, liberty, and the pursuit of happiness. It is used thus, Maritain writes, when we speak of "rights that one possesses and can lay a claim to"[10]—things such as personal rights and property rights. The opposite of right in this sense, W. N. Hohfeld notes, is not "wrong" but "no-right."[11] I have a right to the house that I own, and no right at all to the house that another person owns. Only this second use of right is the proper concern of justice, *i.e.*, of justice understood as a particular virtue distinct from others.

This twofold sense of "right" corresponds to the distinction Aristotle makes between general and particular justice. In the general sense, right includes all that is morally good. The similarity between "right" and "just" in this respect is scarcely surprising in view of the fact that "right" is an English rendering of the Latin word *jus*, from which "justice" is derived.

Maritain proposes the following definition: "A right is a demand or claim (*exigence*) emanating from a self in regard to something as *his* due and which other moral agents are obliged in conscience not to frustrate."[12]

This definition makes it clear that in talking about a right there are at least three elements that have to be taken into account: First, there is an object, something that is due to me in virtue of my possessing such-and-such a right. As the owner of my house, I have the right to privacy, to be secure against trespass, to sell it, or bequeath it, or give it away. The objects in these cases consist in forbearances on the part of others or in actions that I can perform, such as selling or bequeathing. This element Maritain, following Aquinas, calls the *debitum, i.e.*, that which is due.

Second, there is the subject of the right, the agent who possesses it. Thus, I, as the owner of my house, possess the right to it. With respect to this element, a right is something that someone possesses.

Third, there is an obligation laid upon others to respect my right and to observe it either by way of forbearance or of positive action. Thus, corresponding to the possession of a right, there is a correlative duty imposed upon others.

This distinction among three elements in the notion of right serves

10 *Loc. cit.*
11 *Fundamental Legal Conceptions as Applied in Judicial Reasoning and other Legal Essays*, p. 36.
12 *Op. cit.*, pp. 166–167.

to show the equivalence among the three different ways of formulating the Roman definition of justice. We may say of a citizen that he has a *right* to vote, that his vote is *his own* in the sense that it is his own decision and no one else can do it for him, and that it is his *due* as a citizen. These are three ways of talking about the same thing. Any difference is more a matter of emphasis than anything else. Thus it might be claimed that to speak of the vote as a *right* emphasizes its character as a claim or power that the voter enjoys and that others may also possess; to refer to it as *his own* stresses the subject, his possession of it, his property; whereas to speak of it as something that is *due* to him refers most to the obligation that it lays upon others to observe it, the duty that it imposes upon others.

Being but three different ways of referring to one and the same relation, any one of the three terms could serve equally well to formulate the definition of justice. In short, the three formulations are equivalent, and acceptance of any of them as a definition of justice is tantamount to adopting the Natural Right theory of justice. This theory might have been named after either of the other two elements, and one could speak accordingly of the Due theory or the Proprietary theory of justice. Yet it is perhaps more intelligible to call the theory after the element of right. The name then contains a reference to *what is possessed,* and such a reference is perhaps more central to the whole complex notion than one that places the emphasis upon the *fact* of possession, as the term "proprietary" does. So, too, the notion of what is due as a duty seems to be derived from that of right. Furthermore, the relation between the three elements seems to be for most holders of the theory what it is for Maritain. In his definition of right, cited above (p. 125), the other two elements are included. They are, then, for Maritain, somehow logically prior, but, by the same token, this means that the element of right also contains or comprises the other two and thus provides a fuller explication and a more appropriate name for the theory based on it.

All three aspects are present in the notion of right, and what is said about any one of them also touches on the other two. Yet the threefold distinction corresponds roughly to the order we will follow in the exposition of the Natural Right position regarding the fundamental issues of justice. In considering the issues relating to law and society, we will deal primarily with what a right is in itself as a *debitum*. In analyzing the objectivity of justice, we will consider mainly the subject of right, since the nature of man is held to provide the objective basis of justice. Under the obligatoriness of justice, we will deal with the duty that it imposes upon others.

NATURAL RIGHT

We have yet to see, however, how acceptance of the Justinian definition serves to identify a distinctive position regarding the nature of justice. We need to see how right, or due, or what is one's own, can be held to provide a basis for justice that is independent of both the positive law and the social good. This, in turn, will be accomplished once we see how proponents of the position maintain that there is a natural right, a natural justice, such as is denied by both the Social Good theory and the Positive Law theory of justice.

At the risk of repetition, it is worth pointing out again the identifying note of the Natural Right position. It does not lie in the denial that what is just may under certain conditions be identical with what is legal or what serves the common good. To this extent, the Natural Right authors agree respectively with the proponents of the Positive Law theory and the Social Good theory. They go further than this, however, and maintain that there is more to justice than can be caught by the notion of law or of the social good. This additional element is most briefly characterized as natural right—a right that rests ultimately neither on law nor the good of society, but on the nature of man. This natural right is held to be the basic element in justice, underlying both positive law and the social good, and supplying a criterion for them.

The priority of nature, as well as its relation to the other two notions, is affirmed by Cicero when he declares: "Justice has its beginning in nature; then certain things become customary by reason of their utility; still later, both those that came from nature and those approved by custom were sanctioned by the fear of the law and religion."[13]

The order in which Cicero puts the three elements serves to indicate their relative importance in the Natural Right theory of justice: Nature is the most important as providing the basis for justice, which underlies all the other elements; then comes utility,

[13] *De inventione,* II, 53, 160.

understood as what is good for men in their social relations; and, last, as the narrowest, is the positive law.

The assertion of natural right is frequently made in the form of a declaration spelling out a number of specific rights that are claimed to be natural. The American Declaration of Independence asserts that it is a self-evident truth that "all men . . . are endowed by their Creator with certain unalienable rights, that among these are life, liberty, and the pursuit of happiness." The French Declaration of the Rights of Man and of the Citizen claims to enumerate "natural, imprescriptible, and inalienable rights."

In these declarations, as in the writings of many Natural Right authors, the assertion of natural right is often accompanied by certain assumptions and interpretations that do not belong to the minimal agreement of the Natural Right position on justice. Natural rights are sometimes understood as rights that men possess as individuals before they enter into a state of political society; they belong to man in a state of nature prior to civilized life.

Thus Locke, for instance, claims that "all men are naturally in . . . a state of perfect freedom to order their actions and dispose of their possessions and persons as they think fit."[14] This right to live as one likes is not conferred by society or government but belongs to men by nature, and it is natural for men to know and to respect it: "The law of nature . . . which obliges everyone, and reason which is that law, teaches all mankind who will but consult it, that being all equal and independent, no one ought to harm another in his life, health, liberty, or possessions."[15] Locke claims, further, that men, by nature, individually have the right to punish infractions of this basic right of freedom, and that it is relinquished and transferred to society only when individuals freely consent to leave the state of nature and establish a civil society for the purpose of securing such natural rights. Natural right is conceived as belonging to man outside of society as an individual unformed by it. He would say of natural right, as he does of truth and the keeping of faith, that it "belongs to men as men and not as members of society."[16]

To conceive of natural right as belonging to the individual as outside of, and even opposed to, society does not belong to the Natural

14 *Second Treatise of Civil Government,* II, 4.
15 *Ibid.,* II, 6.
16 *Ibid.,* II, 14.

Right position as such. This is an issue on which Natural Right authors divide. T. H. Green states the minimal position that all would agree to when he declares that "rights are innate or natural in the same sense that the state is natural for Aristotle." It is not that "they actually exist when a man is born or have been as long as the human race, but that they are necessary for and arise out of a moral capacity without which a man would not be a man."[17]

Natural rights are also social, since it is only in society that they are claimed, exercised, and acknowledged. A right, as we have seen, imposes an obligation upon someone else to respect and observe it. It is then an interpersonal relationship, and, except in a metaphorical sense, a completely solitary man would have no right. Robinson Crusoe, until the advent of Friday, strictly speaking, enjoyed and exercised no rights upon his island.

But, although it is social, a natural right is not made by and for society. It is not something that exists only for the social good and for the sake of society. It is a human good and exists because of the kind of being man is. This point is made in the minimal way characterizing the general Natural Right position by H. L. A. Hart, when he writes: "This right is one which all men have if they are capable of choice; they have it *qua* men and not only if they are members of some society or stand in some special relation to each other; this right is not created or conferred by men's voluntary action."[18] Although a natural right may exist only in a society of men, a man possesses it because he is a man, and not because he is a citizen or subject of a given society. Although it may arise only through the actions of men associated together, it is not a voluntary power or restriction undertaken solely for the good and interest of society.

The basis of justice in natural right can be asserted in many different ways. Locke's theory of the rights men possess in a state of nature apart from society is only one way. Sometimes the natural basis of justice is asserted by distinguishing natural from conventional justice and claiming that the latter depends on the former. More frequently it is done by distinguishing different kinds of rights and identifying the basic kind as natural, inalienable, personal, or *a priori*.

Aristotle exemplifies the second of these ways. He says that justice

---

[17] *Lectures on the Principles of Political Obligation,* No. 30–31.
[18] "Are There any Natural Rights," in *Philosophical Review,* Vol. 64, 1955, p. 175.

is of two kinds, one natural and the other conventional or legal. "The naturally just is that which has the same power everywhere and does not depend on our accepting it or not, whereas the legally just is that which in the beginning might have been settled indifferently either way, but, once settled, it is no longer indifferent."[19]

Aquinas makes the same distinction in terms of the *debitum*, or of what is owed as a matter of right. The distinction corresponds, he writes, to "those things which are commanded because good and prohibited because bad on the one hand, and to those which are good because commanded and bad because prohibited on the other."[20]

What is naturally just is just in and by itself and does not depend on human agreement. "It is everywhere the same," Aristotle says, "as fire burns both here and in Persia." For him, the most important case of the naturally just is that equals should be treated equally. "That the equal should not go to the equal and the like to the like is contrary to nature," he declares.[21] Men, then, as equals, have a right to equal treatment.

For Aristotle, equality constitutes the basic principle of justice. He does not speak at all of natural right. As Aquinas points out, where the jurists talk of natural and positive right, Aristotle uses the expression the natural and the legal just.[22] What he says about the naturally just and equality shows that he is an adherent of the Natural Right position. This is further confirmed, as we shall see, by his position regarding the relation between justice and law—justice being the wider notion in his account.

Kant, too, upholds the doctrine of natural right. He uses the term, however, in several different though closely related senses, which need to be distinguished. The differences arise from the various opposites with which he contrasts natural right. Natural right is opposed as *a priori* to positive or statutory right. "Natural right rests upon pure rational principles *a priori*; positive or statutory right is what proceeds from the will of a legislator."[23] Elsewhere, he characterizes it as that right "which is knowable purely *a priori* by every man's reason."[24] It therefore continues to exist after the constitution

---

[19] *The Nicomachean Ethics*, 1134b19.
[20] *Op. cit.*, 2–2, 57, 2 ad 3.
[21] *The Politics*, 1325b7.
[22] *In Decem Libros Ethicorum Aristotelis ad Nicomachum Expositio*, No. 1016.
[23] *The Science of Right*, in *Great Books of the Western World*, Vol. 42, p. 401b.
[24] *Ibid.*, p. 429b.

of a civil society. In fact, it supplies a criterion for the positive law in that it "provides the conditions of such a constitution" and therefore is "not to be infringed by the statutory laws of such a constitution."[25]

Natural right is also identified with private right and contrasted with civil or public right.[26] Kant warns expressly that "civil" here is not to be identified with "social." In the state of nature, where only natural right exists, he claims that "there may well be society of some kind, but there is no 'civil' society as an institution securing the *mine* and *thine* by public laws."[27] Natural right in this sense would seem to be identical with all the rights men may have apart from the rights that are specifically public as established by a civil society.

Kant draws still another distinction between what he calls innate right and acquired right. He introduces this distinction by noting that rights may be regarded "in reference to the implied powers of dealing morally with others as bound by obligations." So viewed, he claims that rights may be distinguished as innate or acquired. "*Innate* right is that right which belongs to every one by nature, independent of all juridical acts of experience. *Acquired* right is that right which is founded upon such juridical acts."[28] From this it would appear that innate right is but another way of viewing natural right.

Things, however, are not as simple as this. Kant goes on to claim that there is "only one innate right, the birthright of freedom." This one right he also expresses as consisting in "an innate equality belonging to every man which consists in his right to be independent of being bound by others to anything more than that to which he may also reciprocally bind them." This freedom is further described as "independence of the compulsory will of another . . . in so far as it can coexist with the freedom of all according to a universal law."[29] Furthermore, he claims that innate right "may also be called the 'internal mine and thine,' for external right must always be acquired."[30] But if this is so, it would then seem to follow that all the rights with which justice is concerned are acquired, since right as juridical concerns only *external* objects and actions.

Such a claim introduces considerable complication into the doctrine

25 *Ibid.*, p. 409a.
26 See *ibid.*, p. 402c.
27 *Loc. cit.*
28 *Ibid.*, p. 410b.
29 *Ibid.*, p. 401c.
30 *Ibid.*, p. 401b.

of natural right. As an innate right opposed to acquired rights, it consists of but one right. Yet, as we have seen, natural right is also identified with private right and opposed to public right. This constitutes a large sphere, comprehending many rights. In fact, it is the object of consideration of one of the two main parts into which *The Science of Right* is divided. The full title of this part reads as follows: "Private Right. The system of those laws that require no external promulgation. The principles of the external mine and thine generally."[31] Thus, on the one hand, natural right consists of only one right, the birthright of freedom, while, on the other hand, it consists of many rights, including all those governing real property and contract.

To avoid inconsistency, it would seem that we have to distinguish two kinds of right in natural right itself: using Kant's terms, what we may call an internal and external natural right. With this distinction, it could be claimed that Kant is pointing out what might be described as two different levels of natural right. It is significant that Kant refers to the first in terms of equality as well as of freedom. In fact, the "birthright of freedom" might be viewed as the Kantian way of expressing the basic principle of equality: that equals are to be treated equally, at least when in similar situations. Such a right constitutes the basic criterion of fairness and is certainly of a different order from the right, for example, to private property.

The Kantian texts that we have cited raise several problems that are of special importance for understanding the Natural Right position. One concerns the number of natural rights—whether one or many. Another is the extent to which they are naturally given, and how much they can be specified and detailed in concrete proposals. Involved in this question of specification is the relation of natural right and positive law and the extent to which natural right becomes known only as positively instituted in social institutions and law. Each of these questions constitutes a subissue on which the Natural Right proponents divide. But underlying their differences there is a minimal and general agreement on which all would stand.

All would agree that there is at least one natural right. Those who claim that there is one and only one natural right do not always agree on what it is. Hart agrees with Kant in holding that "if there are any moral rights at all, it follows that there is at least one natural right, the

31 *Ibid.*, p. 403.

equal right of all men to be free."[32] For Stuart M. Brown, however, the "one inalienable right" is the right of all men to institutions protecting their moral interests, persons, and estates.[33] Kant and Hart, explicitly, and Brown, implicitly, assert that this is a right equally possessed by all men. For some authors, equality itself seems to be the predominant right, even if they would not assert that it is the only one. None of the four authors taken as paradigm for the position attempt to enumerate the rights that are natural to man. All would hold that there are several such rights, and one of them, Maritain, would deny that they can ever be exhaustively listed at any one time, since man's knowledge of them is historically conditioned and changes and grows through time. Yet it remains true, nonetheless, that equality, as a principle of justice, figures much more extensively in the Natural Right theory than in any other.

EQUALITY

Among some of the Natural Right proponents, equality is given so prominent a place that they develop what might well be described as an equalitarian theory of justice. Aristotle is the leading representative of this trend, followed by Aquinas and the other writers in the Aristotelian tradition. Locke and Maritain, however, give no more importance to equality than to any other natural right.

"The just," Aristotle writes, "is the lawful and the equal, and the unjust is the unlawful and the unequal."[34] Equality, however, is obviously a different kind of principle from law. It is, by itself, a purely formal principle in that, without further specification, it provides no criterion of relevance or of applicability. It does not say which respects are to count as relevant for consideration in terms of equality. Justice consists in equality, Aristotle claims, but then adds "which equality and which inequality this means is a political question."[35] Men are never equal or unequal in every respect. This fact, Aristotle claims, shows the errors of both democrats and oligarchs. The democrats err in demanding that men should be treated as equal in every respect because they are equal in one, namely, in citizenship.

[32] "Are There Any Natural Rights," p. 175.
[33] "Inalienable Right" in *Philosophical Review*, Vol. 64, 1955, pp. 210–211.
[34] *The Nicomachean Ethics*, 1129b1.
[35] *The Politics*, 1282b21.

The oligarchs err in claiming that, since men are unequal in the one respect of wealth, they should be treated as though they were unequal in every respect. Both are in error, Aristotle maintains, because they overlook the fact that in justice and politics only certain kinds of equality and inequality are relevant. Equality as a principle is thus open to changing and developing conceptions of what is to count as equal.

Although the criterion of relevance may change, it is with respect to the exchange and distribution of material goods that equality is most often proclaimed a principle of justice. In fact, it is in this realm, according to Aquinas, that men first obtain their notion of justice[36] and from which they then extend it to other areas. So, too, for Aristotle, the exchange of goods provides the standard case of justice or injustice. The unjust man, he writes, is the man who "takes more than his share, not of any and all goods, but of those on which good and bad fortune depend."[37]—either more of the good things or less of the bad. Such a man, Aristotle calls "unequal" (*anisos*). In such a situation we would use the word "unfair," but Aristotle's Greek has to make one word do the duty of both "equal" and "fair."

Justice is established, in such a case, when the shares are redistributed so as to bring about an equality. According to Aristotle, the judge originally obtained his name from this activity. The word "*dikaion*," he writes, comes from "*dichaion*," meaning "half," and "the judge is called a 'halver' (*dikast = dichast*) because in dividing the whole into two halves, he gives the people equal parts and, hence, is held to give them their own."[38]

The equality that is involved can be analyzed in terms of a proportion. There are four terms: On the one hand, the persons who are concerned, say *A* and *B*, and, on the other, their respective shares, say *x* and *y*. If *A* = *B*, justice obtains, Aristotle says, only if their shares are also equal, *i.e.*, *x* = *y*. So, too, in cases of exchange, there is justice when the value in goods or services received on each side balances or is equal: the farmer receives for the grapes that he exchanges an equal value in shoes from the shoemaker, and vice versa.

This last example serves to show the need for a criterion of relevance in applying the principle of equality. To obtain an equality in

36 See *Summa Theologica*, 2–2, 58, 11 ad 3.
37 *The Nicomachean Ethics*, 1129b1.
38 *Ibid.*, 1132a28.

exchange, we have to be able to compare the products with one another, *e.g.*, shoes and grapes. We need a standard of measurement. This standard, Aristotle says, is "in reality demand, which holds everything together, since if men cease to have wants, or if their wants alter, exchange will be no longer, or will be on different lines." Money has come to represent demand, and, hence, it is money that "provides the measure which makes things commensurable and reduces them to equality."[39] It supplies the unit which makes grapes commensurable with shoes, beds, houses, and household services. That it can do so, Aristotle claims, is a result of human agreement or convention; he notes that the Greek word for money, *nomisma,* is derived from the word for convention or law, *nomos.*[40] Agreement, or consensus, however, is not limited to the choice of money. It is needed, also, for determining what is to count as equality of demand. The acceptance of the market no less than of money depends on the agreement of men, which is thus implicit in determining what is to count as equal.

Underlying the emphasis upon equality as a basic principle of justice seems to be the presumption that equal treatment among men insofar as they are equal is to be expected and that any departure from it calls for justification. In this sense, the right of equals to equal treatment is what some authors call a prima-facie right, that is, it is one that cannot be denied or taken away without some justification.

William K. Frankena claims that natural rights are inalienable only in the sense that they are prima-facie rights. He denies, in other words, that inalienability means that they are indefeasible and can never be denied or limited without injustice.[41] The fact that one man has or receives more than another does not of itself imply that injustice has been done. Only insofar as men are equal does justice demand that they receive equal treatment. All men are equal before the law as being equally bound by it. They may then justly demand equal treatment when brought to trial before it. But since not all men work equally hard or are equally talented, it is not surprising that not all are equally rewarded. Such inequality is generally admitted to be just, Aristotle says, when justice is meted out according to desert, or merit.

[39] *Ibid.*, 1133b15.
[40] *Ibid.*, 1133a30.
[41] See "Natural and Inalienable Rights" in *Philosophical Review,* Vol. 64, 1955, pp. 228–229.

The justice of inequality based on difference in desert, or merit, is treated by Aristotle as a species of equality. It is, he says, founded on a proportionate, not an arithmetic, equality. Thus, if $A \neq B$, then their shares must not be equal, *i.e.*, $x \neq y$. Hence, when A is greater than B, his share should be greater, and, when he is less than B, his share should be smaller. Injustice occurs, according to Aristotle, only "when equals have and are allotted unequal shares or unequals equal shares."[42]

Not all proponents of the Natural Right theory would agree that the principle of desert can be accommodated under the notion of equality, even granted that an equality of ratios is involved. Some look upon desert, or merit, as a distinct principle, and contrast meritorian with equalitarian justice. Aristotle does not, but this may derive, at least in part, from the fact, already noted, that he makes one word do the work of both "fair" and "equal" (*isos = equal*). All would agree with Aristotle that, in determining what is fair, merit must sometimes be taken into account.

Not even Aristotle, who gives more importance to equality than any other writer on justice, maintains that the notion of justice is fully explained by that of equality. As we have seen, he says expressly that the just is both the equal and the lawful, and he also distinguishes two kinds of justice—one natural, the other legal or conventional.[43] The two pairs would seem to be correlative; at least this is so if "equal" here is understood to refer to the general principle that the equal should go to the equal.[44] There is also, as we have seen, a sense in which the determination of the equal involves a conventional element, especially with regard to what we have called the criterion of relevance.

The Natural Right authors differ with one another regarding the extent to which the natural rights of man can be specified and detailed apart from actual embodiment in social institutions and laws. Some of the Natural Right theorists of the seventeenth and eighteenth centuries, including Jefferson and the founding fathers of the United States, descend to considerable detail in spelling out rights that are claimed to be natural and not the result of social custom and positive

42 *Op. cit.*, 1131a24.
43 See *ibid.*, 1134b18.
44 See *The Politics*, 1325b7.

law. Others are much more restrained and formulate natural right only in terms of the most general principles.

THE CRITERION OF LAW

Differences and disagreements over the number and specification of natural rights reveal differences over the relation between natural right on the one side and society and law on the other. All proponents of the theory would agree, however, that justice provides a criterion of goodness for both society and law. Constitutions, as well as laws, according to Aristotle, "must be good or bad, just or unjust."[45] And he maintains that constitutions can be classified according to their justice, the best state being the one that has "men who are just absolutely and not according to some particular standard."[46]

As the possessor of natural rights, man is not subject to his society in all that he is and has. Not all his rights are conferred by society. Hence, in natural right, he has a basis from which to judge society and its laws. Justice, as rendering to each what is his by natural right, supplies a criterion of both society and law. Justice then, for the Natural Right theory, is not entirely dependent on law.

Yet it must be admitted that some Natural Right authors do claim explicitly that justice always has reference to law. Hooker is typical of these writers when he maintains that "neither God, nor angels, nor men could in any sense be termed just were it not for that which is due to another in regard of some received law between them."[47] But by this he does not mean that justice always refers to positive law. Law, for him, as for many of the Natural Right authors, may be "either natural and immutable or else subject unto change, otherwise called "positive law." These authors, consequently, maintain that justice depends upon law only because they have a much wider notion of law than the one we are using. If the notion of law is restricted to that of positive law, then these authors would admit that justice does not always depend upon law, but, on the contrary, supplies a criterion of law.

According to Aquinas, "laws are written down to declare both natural and positive right."[48] The relation between right and law is

45 *Ibid.*, 1282b8.
46 *Ibid.*, 1228b38.
47 "A Learned Sermon of the Nature of Pride," in *Works*, p. 716.
48 *Op. cit.*, 2–2, 60, 5.

not the same in the two cases. "Written law indeed contains natural right, but it does not institute it, for its force comes, not from the law, but from nature. Written law, however, both contains and institutes positive right, giving it the force of authority." It is significant that Aquinas says the "force [*robur*] of authority." For, by the force or, as we would say, the power of the law, he does not mean the physical force behind the law, *i.e.*, its sanction, but rather its authority to claim obedience merely because it is the law. This authoritative power of the law, according to him, derives from natural right and ceases when the law fails to conform to the right. Thus, he writes, "if the written law contains anything against natural right, it is unjust and does not have the power of obliging." It follows then that if the power of obliging belongs to the essence of law, right and, hence, justice are constitutive elements of law. Enactments contrary to natural right, Aquinas holds "are not to be called laws, but rather corruptions of the law."[49]

Aquinas spells out in still greater detail how a law can be unjust. He specifies three respects in which laws are called just: "From their end, namely when they are ordered to the common good; from their author, when the law laid down does not exceed the power of its maker; from their form, namely when the burdens required by the common good are imposed upon the populace according to a proportionate equality." We have here a set of rules or conditions to which positive laws must conform. A law that fails to meet any of these conditions is unjust and, Aquinas says, "more an act of violence than a law."[50]

It should be noted that only the third of these conditions implies an assertion of natural right as we have been taking it. It asserts that men have a right to be treated equally insofar as they are equal, and unequally insofar as they are unequal, and this right is itself used to measure the law. Hence, it is not itself conferred by law or society. The second condition concerns the form of the law and refers to what is necessary to provide it with legality. This is a condition for justice, which in and by itself would be admitted by the Positive Law theory, since it implies no more than that a law must meet certain rules in order to count as a law. So, too, the first condition, that a law to be just

49 *Ibid.*, 2–2, 60, 5 ad 1.
50 *Ibid.*, 1–2, 96, 4.

must serve the common good, would be allowed by the Social Good theory, since, as we have seen, it constitutes the very basis of justice for this theory. Thus, two of the three conditions that Aquinas names contain nothing belonging peculiarly to the Natural Right position. It is the third of them in this statement that is essential for distinguishing the Natural Right position from that of the other theories. It provides a right men can claim that is not conferred by either law or society—a natural right, then, that can be used to measure both law and society.

Some Natural Right authors, like Locke and Jefferson, hold that many, if not all, natural rights are self-evident. The task of law is, accordingly, merely to secure their observance, since, in the words of the Declaration of Independence, "to secure these rights governments are instituted among men." According to Locke, "a great part of the municipal laws of countries . . . are only so far right as they are founded on the law of nature by which they are to be regulated and interpreted."[51]

For Aquinas and Maritain the relation between the two is much more complex. According to Aquinas, positive laws are related to the natural law in one of two ways: "One way as a conclusion from principles, the other as certain determinations of something more common. The first way is similar to that by which demonstrative conclusions are produced from principles in the sciences. The second is similar to the way that common forms in the arts are determined to something special, as the builder has to determine the common form of a house to this or that figure of a house."[52] Aquinas holds, for example, that both the prohibition against murder and its punishment belong to the natural law, but the first is derived as a conclusion from the principle that evil must not be done, whereas the second is a particular determination made by positive law. These two ways provide Aquinas with a criterion for distinguishing between the law of nations, or *ius gentium,* and the civil law. The law of nations is related to the natural law in the first way, consisting of "those things which are derived from natural law as conclusions from principles, such as just buyings and sellings and the like, without which men could not live together." The civil law consists of "those things which

[51] *Second Treatise of Civil Government,* II, 12.
[52] *Op. cit.,* 1–2, 95, 2.

are derived from natural law by way of particular determination according as each state determines what suits it best."[53]

Maritain, like Kant and Hegel, goes into greater detail than Aquinas to explain how law and social institutions specify, declare, and make known natural right; and, unlike Locke and Jefferson, all three authors regard natural right by itself, apart from social embodiment as more less inchoate in form.

According to Kant, the object of justice is "the external mine and thine"—that is, a rightful claim to something that a person has and that others can be compelled to uphold. For him, obligation and the warrant to compel belong to the very essence of right, and these, he maintains, do not fully exist except in civil society. Hence, Kant does not hesitate to declare that "there can be an external mine and thine only in the civil state of society."[54] Yet he also denies that right is exclusively the product of civil society. Society and its laws only secure effectively and achieve, as it were, what persons in themselves have a natural right to as their own. They guarantee the right. But any "guarantee," Kant writes, "assumes that everyone to whom a thing is secured is already in possession of it as his own. . . . There may thus be a possession in expectation or in preparation for such a state of security, as can only be established on the law of the common will; and as it is therefore in accordance with the possibility of such a state, it constitutes a provisory or temporary juridical possession, whereas that possession which is found in reality in the civil state of society will be a peremptory or guaranteed possession."[55] By natural right, one has "a kind of potential juridical possession," which becomes actual under the law of civil society.

Hegel is notorious for posing a difficult problem of classification. To ask whether right or law is the more primitive term for the analysis of justice is to pose a question that Hegel's whole system of right seems designed to deny; he seems to want to say that both are primitive and need to be reconciled in the higher synthesis he offers. He asserts emphatically that "law and the right are identical"[56]—so much so that his theory of justice is sometimes equated with that of Hobbes,

[53] *Ibid.*, 1–2, 95, 4.
[54] *Op. cit.*, p. 498d.
[55] *Ibid.*, p. 409a–b.
[56] *Philosophy of Right*, No. 211.

thus making him an adherent of the Positive Law position.[57] Yet, on balance, his position seems to come to much the same as Kant's. "Law and the right are identical," Hegel writes, "in the sense that what is implicitly right is posited in the law."[58] But this is to admit that a right can be implicit before it becomes explicit in law. He also admits "the absolute right of appropriation which man has over all things," antecedent to civil society,[59] and grants that the individual and the family have rights even against civil society, although these may be difficult to define.[60] Furthermore, he distinguishes the natural law from positive law and, denying that there is any opposition between them, claims that "the relation is much more like that between *Institutes* and *Pandects*."[61] By this comparison with the basic works of Roman Law, it would appear that Hegel is saying that the natural law is related to positive law as the general to the particular—the *Institutes* being understood to supply the general principles on which the detailed case-law of the *Pandects* is based. In this case, positive law is needed to make particular and concrete what is general and indefinite in the natual law.

According to Maritain, positive laws are "a prolongation or an extension of natural law, passing into objective zones which less and less can be sufficiently determined by the essential inclinations of human nature. For it is natural law itself which requires that whatever it leaves undetermined shall subsequently be determined, either as a right or duty existing for all men and of which they are made aware, not by knowledge through inclination, but by conceptual reason—that's for *ius gentium*—or—and this is for positive law—as a right or duty existing for certain men by reason of the human and contingent regulations proper to the social group of which they are a part."[62]

It is as a complex of natural inclination, conceptual reason, and social patterns and positive law that man has come to know his rights. Among these, Maritain claims that some belong "strictly to the natural law"; he enumerates the "right to existence, to personal freedom, and

---

[57] See Del Vecchio, *Justice: An Historical and Philosophical Essay*, Ch. 11, Note 12, p. 131.
[58] *Loc. cit.*
[59] *Op. cit.*, No. 44.
[60] *Ibid.*, No. 238, A146.
[61] *Ibid.*, No. 3.
[62] *Man and The State*, pp. 99–100.

to the pursuit of the perfection of moral life."[63] These rights provide the basic criterion for judging the justice of positive laws: those are unjust that contravene these basic rights. Maritain does not discuss how one can tell when a law is unjust. He recognizes that concrete situations may give rise to conflict among even these basic rights; it may be necessary, for example, to sacrifice life to preserve freedom. He also admits again that even the most basic rights may have to be limited in their exercise, despite their being inalienable in possession.[64] Hence, in the concrete, it would seem to be no easy task to determine when a given law is definitely contrary to natural law. Perhaps it is only the extreme case that makes it evident, when one's "sense of justice" is outraged and naturally gives rise to a cry for justice.

Although they may differ regarding the relation between natural right and law, all Natural Right proponents agree that justice is a wider notion than law. In this, they agree with the holders of the Social Good position and could appeal to the same arguments (see above, Chapter 5, p. 82). All maintain that questions of justice can arise independent of any question of law.

As evidence for this, Maritain cites two imaginary examples that are worth noting because of the importance they will have later on in connection with the origin of justice. He asks us to imagine the case of an employer who agrees to pay his workers a certain fee and then lives up to his agreement, or the case of a chief of a primitive tribe who is hard and severe, but who treats each member impartially according to his deeds. Here there is no question of law at all. Yet, Maritain claims, "the common man faced with the examples we have been considering would know that the employer or tribal chief are *just* and that to be just is *good*."[65]

These are examples of what Aristotle and Aquinas call commutative and distributive justice—the justice between private individuals and that between the head of a community and its members respectively. There is still another division of justice in Aristotle which provides the theory with further evidence for claiming that justice is wider than law. This consists of what Aristotle calls domestic justice, which is supposed to govern the relations between the various mem-

[63] *Ibid.,* p. 100.
[64] *Ibid.,* p. 101.
[65] *Neuf Leçons,* p. 54.

bers of a household: despotic justice between master and slave, paternal justice between father and child, and conjugal justice between husband and wife.[66] To make such a division of justice amounts to claiming that these domestic relationships give rise to occasions for attributing justice and injustice—cases in which we could speak of a servant being treated unjustly by his master, or cases involving justice and injustice between husband and wife or between parents and children, in all of which there is no question of law.

To hold that justice may be found outside the sphere of law is not to deny that justice may be found most completely within the sphere where law rules. "Justice belongs to the state," Aristotle says, "since as the determination of what is just it is an ordering of the political association."[67] Indeed, Aristotle claims that domestic justice does not realize the notion of justice as completely as political justice. "There can be no injustice in an unqualified sense towards things that are one's own."[68] Therefore, the justice that one does to his slaves and children, and even to his wife, is not as fully and completely justice as that which exists between citizens, *i.e.*, the justice that is "according to law and between people naturally subject to law."[69]

We have now completed our construction of the principal part of the Natural Right position on justice. Although more remains to be done, it may help at this point to summarize our results by listing the propositions all proponents of the theory would accept.

(1) Justice consists in rendering each his right or due.
(2) Right is basic to the notion of justice—right in this case being distinct from right as meaning only what is not wrong.
(3) What is right or due or one's own are equivalent ways of formulating the basis of justice.
(4) Justice is based ultimately on natural right, which men have as men.
(5) There is a natural justice everywhere the same in the sense that there is at least one natural right.
(6) Men have a presumptive right to equality of treatment, insofar as they are equal, any departure from which calls for justification.

[66] See *The Nicomachean Ethics*, 1134b9 ff.
[67] *The Politics*, 1253a37.
[68] *The Nicomachean Ethics*, 1134b9.
[69] *Ibid.*, 1134b12.

(7) Justice provides a criterion of law—a just law being based on natural right.

(8) Justice is a wider notion than that of law, and questions of justice arise independent of questions of law.

THE OBJECTIVITY OF JUSTICE

All Natural Right authors agree that justice is an objective norm of human action. The judgment that X is just is more than a subjective expression of individual approval. It says something objective about X and something more than that X is in conformity with the law or that X is necessary for the social good. In some cases, no more than one or the other of these may be meant, but cases also occur, according to the theory, where X is just means that X is due to man as man; it is something really good as being in accord with his nature and due to him for that reason. Further, the theory also maintains that this meaning is the basic one, since any meaning of justice depending upon either law or the social good cannot ultimately contradict this one. Not all justice may be reducible to natural right, but nothing can be just that is a denial or infraction of that right. What is just is approved as good, the theory maintains, because it is ultimately seen to be a good for man; the approbative character of justice has a natural basis.

The assertion of the objectivity of justice is seen most clearly in the discussion of how men come to know what is naturally just, or, more generally, of the basis of fundamental moral principles. On this subject there is great diversity of opinion among the Natural Right authors.

All four of our paradigm authors hold that knowledge of moral principles is a form of rational knowledge. All four, in fact, speak of the "practical principles" of reason in referring to knowledge of what ought to be done in the sphere of action or practice. But, for some Natural Right authors, the grasp of moral principle and, hence, of what is naturally just, is not ultimately based on rational knowledge. Jefferson holds that we know natural right by means of "a special moral sense—a sense as much a part of man as feeling, seeing, hearing."[70] According to Brentano, man has a natural insight, a

[70] *Jefferson to Adams*, October 14, 1816, Vol. 16, p. 76.

natural preference for what is ethical, which is neither an innate principle nor a feeling of compulsion.[71]

Locke denies that there are any "innate practical principles," and yet affirms that it is certain that there is a natural law "and that as intelligible and plain to a rational creature and a studier of that law as the positive laws of commonwealths, nay, possibly plainer; as much as reason is easier to be understood than the fancies and intricate contrivances of men following contrary and hidden interests put into words."[72] In his early *Essays on the Law of Nature,* he equates this law with the moral good or virtue of the Stoics and with right reason as well as with the will of God, and claims that men can attain to knowledge of it through reasoning from sense experience.[73] He also denies expressly that it is identical with the private and subjective interest of the individual. Hence, too, the rules of natural justice falling under the natural law are objective.[74]

For Aquinas, the natural moral judgments of man are based on his inclinations toward objects that he sees as naturally good. "Since the good has the nature of end," he writes, "all to which man has a natural inclination is truly apprehended by reason as good." He distinguishes three basic inclinations: "The first is the inclination for the good that man naturally shares with all substances, namely for the conservation of his being according to the nature that he has. . . . The second is an inclination for something more special according to the nature that he shares with other animals . . . for the union of male and female, the education of children, and the like. The third is the inclination in man for the good of the rational nature proper to him; hence man has a natural inclination to know the truth about God and to live in society . . . and what pertains to these, such as to avoid ignorance and offending those with whom he lives."[75]

Since these are the ends man is inclined to because of the kind of being he is, he has a natural right to what is necessary for the attainment of them. Natural rights, John A. Ryan writes, "are the moral means or opportunities by which the individual attains the end appointed to him by nature. . . . necessary means of right and reasonable living . . . so necesssary and so sacred that all other

---

[71] See *The Origin of the Knowledge of Right and Wrong,* No. 4, 8, 20.
[72] *Second Treatise,* II, 12.
[73] *Essays on the Law of Nature,* pp. 109–111, 147.
[74] See *ibid.,* pp. 205 ff.
[75] *Op. cit.,* 1–2, 94, 2.

persons than the one in whom they reside are morally restrained from interfering with or ignoring them."[76] With respect to such goods or means, it is naturally just that others should recognize my right and that I should recognize theirs.

Aquinas refers, as we have seen, to natural inclinations. The moral judgments about them are based on what he calls the first principle of practical reason. They are the work of reason, but of a reason that is practical as concerning what ought to be done. The first principle, which, as first, is self-evident, *i.e.*, evident immediately to anyone understanding the terms, is that the good is to be done and evil avoided. As self-evident, it does not need to be reasoned to; it is seen at once and, in this sense, is intuited. Yet Aquinas also maintains that other natural moral judgments are inferred as conclusions from this first principle as premise. As an example, he claims that the precept "Do not kill" is drawn as a conclusion from the principle "Harm no man," which he evidently considers as a particularization of the general principle "Do no evil." What is seen as naturally good in this case is a work of reasoning or of drawing conclusions from prior premises.

Aquinas is seldom more specific than this about the actual content of natural law. He does say in his analaysis of the Ten Commandments that "the second table [the last five] contains the order of justice to be observed among men, namely that each is to be rendered his due and nothing undue is to be done to anybody."[77] Yet he talks at times as though all the Ten Commandments, except keeping holy the Sabbath Day, belong to the natural law. And he also claims that the knowledge of the natural law has become so obscured by sin that God has instituted His law so that man may know his own natural good.[78]

Maritain is even more reserved than Aquinas in actually specifying man's natural goods. He expressly criticizes the claims of the Natural Law theorists of the seventeenth and eighteenth centuries, and holds that "one of the main errors of the rationalist philosophy of human rights has been to regard positive law as a mere transcript traced off from natural law, which would supposedly prescribe in the name of nature all that which positive law prescribes in the name of society."[79]

[76] *A Living Wage,* pp. 76, 78.
[77] *Op. cit.,* 1–2, 100, 8.
[78] See *ibid.,* 1–2, 98, 6.
[79] *Man and the State,* p. 97.

He finds only one principle that he claims clearly belongs to the natural law and is known certainly by all men, namely, the principle that we must do good and avoid evil, and this, he says, is "the preamble and the principle of the natural law; it is not the natural law itself." For him, the natural law consists of "the ensemble of things to do and not to do which follow therefrom in a necessary fashion."[80]

According to Maritain, moral principles are first known by knowledge through inclination. This is obtained in and through the concrete situation, and, hence, though it may be rooted in nature, it is manifested only in history. "All our concepts of the practical order," Maritain writes, "have a signification that is both rational and historical," and even though the rational sense is the essential object of our search, it is as it were embedded in the historical.[81] To know what is meant by knowledge through inclination we have to look to the concrete. Maritain offers the imaginary examples, cited earlier, which involve the idea of justice.

He asks us to imagine a man without ethical sophistication or reflection, who finds himself in the presence of a man who pays his workers an agreed upon salary, or before the chief of a primitive tribe who is hard and severe, but who treats each member impartially according to his deeds. "Faced with such examples as these," Maritain claims, "reason experiences a certain pleasure, it feels content and at home."[82] Although this is a rational experience, he claims that it is not abstract and conceptualized or verbalized. "The situation in question is apprehended in a certain view or concrete notion of reason which remains engaged, immerged, incarnated in the situation itself, inseparable from it and in a preconscious state that is not expressed in a mental word, but which, if it were translated into abstract terms, would yield something like 'render to each what is due to him.' "[83] Implicit in this experience, he says, are two aspects that can be distinguished: "First, the view that the man in question, in acting as he does, is treating the others as men; the philosopher would say that treating men not as things but as persons is one of the essential finalities of human nature. And secondly, as a consequence of this, the view or feeling that such conduct is in accord with something true that we bear within us, or as the philosopher would say, with rea-

80 *Ibid.*, p. 90.
81 *Neuf Leçons*, p. 23.
82 *Ibid.*, p. 51.
83 *Ibid.*, pp. 51–52.

son."[84] In other words, Maritain is claiming that we discover what responses to make in the situations that call them forth; we find what we ought to do, hence, apprehend moral rules, only through being in the particular situation of the sort in question.

Maritain goes on to say that this nonconceptual yet rational experience offers "a point of convergence or fixation which places in movement corresponding inclinations and emotions, as for example satisfaction and sympathy in the above case."[85] Out of these inclinations, and according to them, Maritain claims that "conscious reason, reason functioning as reason, comes to make spontaneously its value judgments. Our intelligence does not judge in virtue of arguments and of conceptual connections, of demonstrations and logical constraints, it judges in a non-conceptual fashion by conformity to the inclinations that are in us and without being able to express the reasons for its judgment."[86] Such knowledge by inclination is said to constitute "our natural knowledge of ethical values." It is the way that "the common man faced with the example we have been considering would know that the employer or tribal chief are *just* and to be just is *good*."[87] The notion of justice is "implicitly present"; it can be made explicit and expressed. But it is "first expressed in social patterns rather than in personal judgments."[88] Hence, Maritain claims that knowledge of the natural law "has developed within the double protecting tissue of human inclinations and human society."[89] Furthermore, being historically conditioned, it is susceptible of development and progress. "Once moral judgments are consciously made they can themselves become the source of inclinations and secondary tendencies; the dynamism of inclinations becomes progressively richer and new typically moral tendencies will arise, depending upon the notion of values explicitly formulated which will find expression in praise or blame, approbation, indignation, etc."[90] Reflection and conceptualization, as well as accumulated experience, contribute to increasing purification of our understanding of moral principles and, hence, too, of the notion of justice.

[84] *Ibid.*, p. 52.
[85] *Loc. cit.*
[86] *Ibid.*, pp. 53–54.
[87] *Ibid.*, p. 54.
[88] *Man and the State*, p. 92.
[89] *Loc. cit.*
[90] *Neuf Leçons*, pp. 54–55.

In this example there are two points that all Natural Right authors would agree to—two points, then, that serve to characterize the position as such. The first is that, given the nature of the case presented in the example, men in any society would naturally recognize the just act; and the second is that they would approve of it as good. Both the judgment and the approbation, while they may involve feeling and emotion, are not limited to these. They have an objective basis, which is independent of the individual's feeling of approval. Natural right provides the ultimate basis and is itself based on the nature of man, which is open to all to see, and which is shared by all men. Frankena speaks for the whole tradition when he writes, "All men have certain rights and they have them simply because they are capable of choice, of reason, of happiness and unhappiness, or because of some other characteristic which they all have."[91]

All proponents of the theory hold that there is a norm for what is due to man, which is natural as well as moral—natural as based on what man is, and moral as obliging one to the observance of it. As we have seen in analyzing the Social Good theory, some writers claim that it is contradictory to assert that something is at once natural and moral, and, more particularly, that to argue from a natural property to a moral obligation is to commit a fallacy—the so-called naturalist fallacy. We will have to consider this objection in some detail when we come to analyze further the obligatory character of justice. But, for the moment, we need only note that the natural, for this theory, is opposed to the conventional and not to the moral, that is, to what is the work of positive enactment by men in society. What is due to man as a matter of right, and, hence, the object of justice, is based, first, on the nature of man. This is not to deny that some, if not most, of the particular rights that men may enjoy are the result of agreement among men in society. But, although the positive rights may be more numerous, the natural are the more basic, in that the positive are held to depend upon them.

To claim that there is a natural due and right is to assert that it is possible to find, by considering the nature of man, an order of goods that are due him. As Locke puts it, "there is a fixed and permanent rule of morals which reason itself pronounces and which persists, being a fact so firmly rooted in the soil of human nature . . . since

[91] "Natural and Inalienable Rights," in *Philosophical Review,* Vol. 64, 1955, p. 224.

man has been made such as he is, equipped with reason and his other faculties and destined for this mode of life, there necessarily result from his inborn constitution some definite duties for him, which cannot be other than they are."[92]

The assertion of natural right does not presuppose, as has been noted, a state of nature, either historical or hypothetical, in which men live apart from and prior to their coming together and being ruled by positive laws. Some Natural Right authors, such as Locke, for example, do make use of such a notion. Others do not. So, too, the assertion of natural right does not necessarily presuppose that man must be taken in the solitary state as an individual opposed to a social life in common with others, although Kant, for example, does speak of natural rights as personal and distinguishes them from public rights.

The pertinent fact, for the theory, is the kind of being that man is. He has such dignity that what is ultimately due him is logically prior to any social agreement or public enactment or institution. According to Maritain, "the good that is involved in a right is *due to me* because I am an I, a self [*un je, un soi*]." This serves to distinguish man from animal, which "has no self, no interior world which appears as his possession." Unlike man, the animal is not a person. "The fact of holding oneself in hand, the possession of self by self is a specific characteristic of the person." With this, according to Maritain, "the notion of the due is transfigured; it signifies now something which is due to my self [*à mon moi*], to my person as *its* due. The good due is *mine* even before I have it, and even if I do not have it. It belongs to the sphere of my possession of myself by myself, to the sphere of what the self possesses."[93]

Among the Natural Right theories of justice, there is little analysis of the abstract meaning of due as such. It is much more common to find discussions of particular rights and duties. Yet it is possible to find certain assumptions about the due which are commonly accepted.

Maritain is the only one of our paradigm authors to analyze the meaning of *debitum*. He starts from the notion of privation in the physical and nonethical order, such as lameness. This, he says, is a privation not a simple negation, since it comes from "a lack, from an absence in muscular connection, or in the proportion of the bones, or

---

[92] *Essays on the Law of Nature,* p. 199.
[93] *Op. cit.,* p. 165.

in nervous energy." The lame animal lacks "a good that is *due,* a good that *should be* present," since an animal "is made to move." Hence, when it is lame, it lacks "what is due to it in light of the natural finality of the organism . . . the lack of a certain good, of a certain being which *should be* present, which is unconditionally required by a thing in virtue of its nature: *privatio boni debiti.*"[94]

Thus, implicit in the notion of the due is that of a good that is owed to something, that should be there. But, Maritain emphasizes, there is nothing moral about the *should* at this stage. Lameness, a toothache, death—each is a privation, an evil, but not a moral evil; the due is not a moral due. "Not being a moral due, there is no implication of any moral obligation," and, hence, Maritain claims, no question of justice or injustice. It is not until we reach the distinctly human order of freedom and value that there is any possibility of moral evil, right, and justice—not, that is, until we have human agency and responsibility.

In this, Maritain is claiming that the due of justice arises only where there is human freedom and responsiblity; a sphere, then, that is coterminous with the moral order. Cases can occur in which a man is responsible for causing a toothache, lameness, death, in another person and then, of course, questions of justice would arise. Maritain's examples are to be understood of those cases in which man is not responsible—as happening, perhaps, to a wild beast in the jungle. Here we are "simply confronted with a privation of an ontological good which should be present. . . . It is not the privation of a good which would be morally due a person from another person."[95] Hence, for Maritain, there is not in the mere fact of natural privations, such as death, blindness, pain, ground for speaking of the injustice of nature or of God. Not all authors, even among adherents to the naturalist theory, would agree with this. But this is a side issue, away from the main point on which all would agree, namely, that there is a norm for what is due to man and that it is both natural and moral.

THE OBLIGATORINESS OF JUSTICE

We have already seen from our initial analysis of right that obligation is one of its essential elements or aspects. A right by the very fact of being a right obliges others to respect it. This much would

94 *Ibid.,* p. 45.
95 *Ibid.,* p. 46.

be agreed to by all proponents of the Natural Right theory. Thus, Maritain declares, "the person who possesses a right is not only in the presence of things which are themselves his due, but also in the presence of other moral agents who are morally obliged, bound in conscience, not to deprive that person of the things in question."[96] The right itself is, as he sees it, the good or value that one is obliged to respect: "The duty or obligation is not first and before all towards the possessor of a right, but purely and simply towards the good, and above also the duty to avoid what is evil," and the obligation to the person as the possessor of the right has to take second place, as it were, after the realization that "it would be bad not to recognize his right."[97]

When one goes on to ask why one ought to do what is just by respecting the right of another, the characteristic answer of the Natural Right theory is that one ought merely because it is good and just. No further justification is needed: Seeing what is just carries with it the obligation to do it. According to this theory, not only are there things that are naturally just but there is also a natural obligation to do them.

Thus, Locke, after noting that the jurists define obligation as "the bond of law whereby one is bound to render what is due," declares that the law in question here must be "the bond of natural law whereby one is bound to discharge a natural obligation, that is, to fulfill the duty which it lies upon one to perform by reason of one's nature."[98] Although he traces the law back to the will of God, he also says that it is "not fear of punishment, but a rational apprehension of what is right, that puts us under an obligation."[99]

Aquinas maintains that the principles of justice are naturally right, independent of positive law, and attributes their naturalness to the social nature of man: "Those things without which human society could not exist are naturally fitting to man, and such are the principles that one should render to each his own and not injure another."[100]

Aristotle, has nothing to say directly about obligation. But he does say that "the good man does what he ought, since intelligence always chooses for itself that which is best, and the good man obeys his

96 *Ibid.,* p. 166.
97 *Ibid.,* pp. 152–153.
98 *Essays on the Law of Nature,* p. 181.
99 *Ibid.,* p. 185.
100 *Contra Gentiles,* 3, 129.

intelligence."[101] And, among goods, the best is the virtuous good (*bonum honestum*), which is superior to pleasure (*bonum delectabile*), because nobler; and better than the useful (*bonum utile*), because an intrinsic good, which is good in itself and not merely good as a means to a further end.[102]

According to the Natural Right theory, there is no need to appeal to the social good or to the sanction of law to account for the obligatoriness of justice; one need only appeal to the conscience of men. The judgment may be aided and reinforced by social institutions, but these of themselves are not sufficient to explain why one ought to be just. This obligation has its basis in the moral nature of man. Thus Ryan writes, "these primary and general moral intuitions produce in the mind of the person who heeds them the conviction that it is not only reasonable but obligatory for him to pursue the path of conduct thus dimly outlined."[103]

Natural Right authors agree that justice imposes a distinct obligation, a moral *ought* not to be confused with any others, such as the teleological, the punitive, or the approbative *ought*. But they differ in their accounts of moral obligation. There are those, like Kant, who make moral duty a categorical imperative; one must be just because it is one's duty. For others, like Aristotle and Aquinas, being just is linked to the ends of human nature, and to be unjust is to thwart and frustrate man's purpose as man. For still others, like Locke, one must do one's duty because it is the will of God.

To appeal to the ends to which man is by nature inclined as a basis for justice seems to some to commit what is sometimes called the naturalist fallacy. It is as though one were to argue that because man *is* such-and-such, he *ought* to act in this way and no other. To have an *ought* in the conclusion, one has to have at least one *ought* in the premises; no number of *is*-statements by themselves can validly yield a moral *ought*, and to argue as though they could is to commit a fallacy—as though an ethical conclusion could be derived from non-ethical premises.

From the name of the theory, one might think that the Natural Right position on justice is peculiarly subject to the naturalist fallacy. Some authors do have little to say about the source of obligation and

[101] *The Nicomachean Ethics*, 1169a15.
[102] See *ibid.*, 1155b19 ff.
[103] *Op. cit.*, p. 78.

seem to make it depend directly on the kind of being that man is. The Natural Right position as such, however, is not necessarily guilty of the fallacy, although few Natural Right authors explicitly say anything about it.

At first it may look as though the Natural Right position derives the ethical proposition that men have rights that ought to be respected from the descriptive and nonethical observation that men have such-and-such a nature. Frankena argues, however, that the position "does not involve deducing 'All men have inalienable rights' from 'All men have the nonethical property *P*' alone," since to obtain the required conclusion it also has the help of an additional ethical premise that "All beings with the property *P* have inalienable rights. The traditional theory, when it says that all men have right *R* because they have the property *P* is not saying that having *R* entails having *P*, but only that having *P* is a sufficient condition of having *R*."[104]

Aquinas, as we have seen, claims that the "first principle of the practical order" is given in the precept: "The good is to be done, evil to be avoided." In saying that this principle belongs to the practical order, he is explicitly distinguishing it from the theoretical order and thus, in effect, noting that it is concerned with an *ought* and not an *is*. This principle is not merely a descriptive statement to the effect that men do act for what they look upon as good, but is an ethical and normative statement that men ought to do what is really good for them as in line with human nature. Aquinas does, at times, speak as though this principle were merely descriptive, especially when he uses it as a cosmic principle and applies it analogously to all that is. It then seems to amount to no more than that things do pursue what they grasp as good. But, when he is speaking of men only, as he is in dealing with natural right and law, he is within the practical or ethical order. The principle can, accordingly, be formulated strictly as a precept, that is, as a command: "Do good and avoid evil," or as the corresponding *ought* statement: "Men ought to do good and avoid evil." It is a directive principle.

Further, in calling it a "first principle," Aquinas is also claiming that it is known immediately, and not discursively as a conclusion of reasoning. It is the first principle of "practical reason," and thus not incompatible or opposed to reason.

Maritain talks explicitly in terms of "norms." He distinguishes

104 *Op. cit.*, pp. 224–225.

three kinds, which he calls *norme-pilote*, *norme-precepte*, and *norme-contrainte*, and which I shall translate, respectively, as guiding-norm, obliging-norm, and constraining-norm. The one we are most interested in is the obliging-norm, since it carries the note of obligation, but Maritain maintains that it cannot be understood apart from the guiding-norm. This he compares to a ruler for drawing straight lines or a compass for drawing circles. Here there is no question of obligation, yet, if we would obtain a true straight line or circle, each being what it should be, then, he says, we have to follow these guiding-norms. The guiding- and obliging-norm, he says, are "extremely close to each other," and he notes that the word "order" has two correspondingly close senses, as disposition or arrangement and as command.[105]

Obligation is described as "a result in us, a consequence of the value of the act, but the value, the moral goodness of the act, depends upon the norm or the rule in the sense of guiding-norm, as implying conformity to this rule." Maritain claims that the obliging-norm derives from the guilding-norm "so normally that the two senses are generally confused," but he insists that, of the two, "the first sense is the more essential, the more fundamental, since it is the norm in this sense that enters into the very constitution of the moral good."[106] The obliging-norm "comes to light for the most part from extra-philosophical factors, whether social or religious." Yet it plays a no less essential role. "Our conscience exhorts us, reproaches us, commands us; and this essential role played by the obliging-norm depends on the first principle of synderesis: the evil is to be avoided, the good is to be done, you must do good, you must avoid evil. What is bad—in comparison with the norm as measure—is prohibited by the norm as precept."[107]

Maritain, no less than Aquinas, passes from the natural to the moral order. He might also be said to be using the same means for avoiding the naturalistic fallacy. The "first principle of synderesis" introduces the *ought* and the sense of impulsion and urgency. Yet it should be noted that Maritain explicitly refuses to make the sharp division between the descriptive and the normative that some philosophers do. An I.Q. score, which certainly seems to be a descriptive psychological

[105] *Neuf Leçons*, p. 134.
[106] *Ibid.*, p. 135.
[107] *Ibid.*, p. 139.

statement of certain abilities of a person, is for him a normative statement, a value judgment, although presumably only as a guiding-norm.[108] It is not a moral statement, as implying obligation, and does not possess the impulsive power of an *ought*. However, to define the moral good, Maritain demands more than just an *ought*. There are, as it were, two moments or two parts to his argument. First, there is the apprehension of what is good for man, which consists in conformity with the guilding-norm of reason; then, second, the application of the principle that what is good ought to be done. The obligation, the *ought*, enters with the second moment. But, because of its dependence on the first moment, it is not blind. Thus Maritain expressly denies that there is any "moral *intuition* as through some sixth sense, or a moral *sentiment* as through a revelation of nature."[109] He claims that "the feeling of obligation is the feeling of being *bound* by the good that I *see*. . . . It is a constraint not at all physical, but purely intellectual, a constraint of the vision upon the will in virtue of the very nature of the will, consisting in this that I would be *bad* if I did such an act and that I cannot will to be bad, as tending to what is evil as evil."[110]

By "constraint" here Maritain means no more than a sense of propulsion, and not at all something difficult to do. This element enters only with what he calls the *constraining-norm* and is "due to the existential condition of man" as a fallen and evil creature. "If I am bad, and if the obliging-norm commands me to be good, it is not only a commandment, which appears as a law of constraint."[111]

The obliging-norm, according to Maritain, imposes an obligation that is categorical. It is not conditional or hypothetical as depending upon an end to be pursued, which is to say that it is not of the form: "If you want that, you must do this." For, if this were so, then the last end of man would not be unconditionally obligatory upon him. It is rather the other way around: "It is not to attain my end that I am obliged, unconditionally obliged, with regard to my supreme end; it is because this end has a supreme value that I am morally obliged with regard to it."[112] This is to emphasize again that it is only to value or a good apprehended that obligation can pertain. Hence, the primacy of

108 See *ibid.*, p. 44.
109 *Ibid.*, p. 58.
110 *Ibid.*, pp. 154–155.
111 *Ibid.*, p. 140.
112 *Ibid.*, p. 84.

value, which leads Maritain to claim that the obliging-norm depends on the guiding-norm.

The subordination of constraint shows the relative unimportance of the notions of force and of sanctions in Maritain's conception of the duty of justice. Justice as a social and moral norm is obligatory on its own; it imposes a moral duty that ought to be obeyed even in the absence of sanctions, even if one possessed the ring of Gyges and could be as unjust as one pleased without ever being detected.

The Natural Right position does not deny that the duty of justice may be enforced by the sanctions of law and of society. Authors as diverse as Aristotle and Kant maintain that justice concerns an external, objective act, and the just act may be done entirely from compulsion and fear of the consequences. The act of justice, Kant writes, regards "the external and practical relation of one person to another in so far as they can have influence upon each other, immediately or mediately, by their actions as fact"; it has nothing to do with "the wish or mere desire of another, as in acts of benevolence," or with his intention.[113] The just act, in this case, however, is not the act of a just man, since it does not proceed from the virtue of justice; it is legal only and not moral.

JUSTICE AND THE MORAL GOOD

According to the Natural Right theory, justice is a distinct virtue, and there is no tendency to confuse it with either obedience or benevolence. For Aristotle, justice is one of the four cardinal virtues. Like other moral virtues, it is a habit of conduct; but, unlike courage and temperance, it is a habit of action and not of the passions. It is that settled inclination "in virtue of which the just man is said to be a doer, by choice, of that which is just, and one who will distribute either between himself and another or between two others not so as to give more of what is desirable to himself and less to his neighbor, and conversely with what is harmful, but so as to give what is equal in accordance with proportion."[114]

Also unlike the other moral virtues, the act of justice can be decided without reference to the agent. How much a person can drink without

[113] *The Science of Right*, in *Great Books of the Western World*, Vol. 42, p. 397c–d.
[114] *The Nicomachean Ethics*, 1134a1–6.

being intemperate depends on the person, but what one owes the bartender depends on how much has been drunk. Hence, Aquinas says, justice is the only virtue that implies the notion of the *debitum*, of what is due to another.[115] He therefore finds, as we have seen, the Roman definition satisfactory for characterizing justice as a virtue: "Justice is the constant and perpetual will to render to each his right." As he interprets it, the voluntary character that is demanded of any virtue is shown by the word "will" (*voluntas*). The firmness or stability demanded of a virtue, which distinguishes it from a passing whim or impulse, is signified by the words "constant and perpetual," where "perpetual" indicates the will always to observe justice, while "constant" indicates firm perseverance in it. The "proper matter and object" of justice is given in the words, "rendering to each his right," about which enough has already been said.[116]

Not all adherents of the Natural Right theory would agree with Aquinas in his analysis of virtue. But all would agree that the virtue of justice cannot be simply identified with obedience to law. Of course, there are occasions when such an identification is correct, *i.e.*, when the just coincides with the legal. But, as we have seen, this is by no means the whole story of justice for this position.

The connection of obedience with justice is analyzed by Aquinas in terms of what, following Cicero, he calls the "virtues annexed to justice," *i.e.*, virtues which agree with a principal virtue in some respects but fall short of it in others.[117] Obedience in this sense is part of justice, but is not identical with it.

The Social Good authors, as we have seen, feel the need to prevent justice from being assimilated to benevolence. The Natural Right authors have a comparable need to keep justice from becoming identified or confused with the whole of virtue. Ordinary discourse sometimes uses "just" and "right" as though they were the same as "morally good." The Just One, for example, is the man who is all good—good in having all the virtues and not merely the virtue of rendering each his due, or, as the Greek proverb puts it, "In justice is all virtue found in sum."[118]

Plato's discussion of justice in *The Republic*, as we have already

---

[115] *Op. cit.*, 1–2, 99, 5 ad 1.
[116] See *ibid.*, 2–2, 58, 1.
[117] See *ibid.*, 2–2, 80, 1.
[118] *Nicomachean Ethics*, 1129b30.

noted (above, pp. 70–71), becomes, in effect, a concern for the moral good as such, raising such questions as why a person should be virtuous, and whether there is an intrinsic reason apart from the possiblity of external sanctions. Aristotle, too, notes that there is a justice that is not a part but rather the whole of virtue as directed toward the good of others.[119] But then he also argues that justice in another sense is but a part of virtue, distinct in itself from all others; and his own theory of justice, once he has made this distinction between the two, is devoted entirely to the analysis of particular justice as one virtue among many.[120]

Aquinas adopts this Aristotelian distinction and develops it in a way that sometimes leads to confusion. He distinguishes the general virtue of justice from the special virtue according as it directs men to the common good of society rather than in relation to an individual man.[121] But, then, since "it belongs to law to direct things to the common good," he also calls this general justice by the name of "legal justice" and says that it is particularly needed by the ruler to enable him "to direct the actions of all the virtues to the common good."[122]

The term "legal justice" used in this way can readily give rise to serious misunderstanding. Aristotle, as we have seen, speaks of legal justice as distinct from natural justice. But when it is so taken to mean only the justice established by positive law, it becomes identical with the Positive Law position that this is the only kind of objective justice there is. Of course, in this sense, the adjective "legal" has little function, except to rule out subjective uses of "justice." But more serious difficulty arises when it is asked whether "legal justice" involves anything more than legality or lawfulness. This constitutes an issue even among the Natural Right theories. It is posed by the question, whether legal justice is to be identified with obedience to authority. On this issue some Natural Right authors take an affirmative position, while others hold the negative.[123]

The affirmative answer to this question poses a serious difficulty for a naturalist author, since he then seems to hold that positive law justly can demand absolute obedience for itself. But this is to assume that

---

119 See *ibid.*, 1130a9; 1130b20.
120 See *ibid.*, 1130b30.
121 See *op. cit.*, 2–2, 58, 5 and 7.
122 *Ibid.*, 2–2, 58, 5 and 6.
123 See Arthur Utz, *Ethique Sociale*, pp. 139–58, for a report on this controversy among the theologians.

cases can arise when the positive law is not to be measured and judged by the higher criterion that justice provides—which is contrary to the basic naturalist position that justice is ultimately prior to the state. The difficulty would seem to arise from the ambiguity underlying the assertion that what is legal is just. The Natural Right theory would admit this only with the further proviso that the law in question is itself just.

With this we have completed the Natural Right theory of justice. We can sum up our results in the following identifying propositions. To facilitate comparison with the other basic theories, they are enumerated, not in the order of exposition, but in that of the fundamental issues.

(1) Justice is a wider notion than that of law, inasmuch as questions of justice arise independent of questions of law.

(2) Justice provides a criterion of law—a just law being one that is based on or not contrary to natural right.

(3) Justice consists in rendering to each his right or due.

    Right is basic to the notion of justice and is distinct from right as meaning what is not wrong.

    What is right or due or one's own are equivalent ways of formulating what is just.

    There is at least one natural right, determined by the nature of man and not by social or legal enactment.

    Men have a presumptive right to equality of treatment insofar as they are equal.

(4) Justice is an objective norm for human action based on what is due man as a man.

    The approbation of justice has an objective basis and is not merely an individual's subjective feeling.

(5) Justice imposes a moral duty to render to each his due.

    The moral obligation of justice is not entirely or exclusively dependent on legal and social sanctions.

(6) Justice is a distinct virtue, disposing one to render to each his due.

    Justice is a special virtue not to be confused with virtue as such.

III

The Shape
of the
Controversy

7

The Three-Sided Controversy
About Justice

THE main part of our task has now been completed. We have considered in detail each of the three basic theories of justice by analyzing and describing the position taken on the six issues that we found to be fundamental in the discussion of justice. These issues were obtained, it will be recalled, as a result of identifying three common notes about justice that are accepted by all and that serve, accordingly, to establish a common subject of controversy.

In the course of analyzing the basic theories in the last three chapters, we have had occasion to point out how each theory differs from the others and where it agrees and disagrees with them. But for the most part the comparison of the theories with each other has been kept to a minimum and utilized mainly for making clear the position of the theory being discussed. Up to now the controversy as a whole has not been the direct subject of attention, except in the preliminary work of the first part. We could not bring the three basic theories fully into confrontation with one another until we had seen where each stood on the fundamental issues. Now that that has been accomplished, we can consider the shape of the controversy as a whole, note the leadiing arguments each theory offers against the other two, and thus map in greater detail than has been possible before the agreements and disagreements among the three and where the issues have been joined in the three-sided controversy about justice.

THE RELATIVE COMPLEXITY OF THE THEORIES

Each of the three basic theories, has, as we have seen, its own privileged term for the analysis of justice. There is, in each case, one term that is claimed to provide the best and fullest explanation of justice in its more important senses and the basis for the most adequate definition of justice. We find accordingly that justice is defined in three different ways as:

> conformity to the law,
> doing what is useful for the social good,
> rendering to each what is his own or due by right.

The first of these definitions, as it is developed by the Positive Law theory, is the simplest of the three. It is also a different kind of definition from the other two. In claiming that justice consists in nothing more than conformity to the law, the theory reduces the just to the legal and comes close to maintaining that justice in both word and notion could to all intents and purposes be eliminated without loss. When it comes to saying anything really important and objectively significant, anything that we do with "just" could be done equally well, according to this theory, with the word "legal." While it cannot be denied that justice is frequently referred to as though it meant something more than legality, the theory claims that in such usage "justice" ceases to have any objective meaning and is purely subjective. Thus, as we have seen, the Positive Law theory consists of two distinct claims: first, that justice as an objective norm is identical with legality; and, second, that justice in any other sense is not objectively meaningful. The second point involves a theory of the meaning of normative and value terms. Justice is admitted to be a complex notion, but, on this view of it, the complexity results from the compounding of objective and subjective uses of the term. In the objective sense, which is the important one, justice is held to consist simply in legality.

This view of justice is the simplest of the three for still other reasons. The scope of justice is more restricted, since it will apply only to actions that are measured by positive law; it will not apply to the law itself as it does on the two other theories. Then, too, there are agreed upon and public ways of resolving differences over justice when it consists only in determining whether or not an action is in accord with the law, since it is for this very purpose that courts of law and judges have been established.

Still another sign that the Positive Law theory is the least complex of the three appears in the fact that it has the smallest number of variants. There is less to disagree about, hence fewer special issues to give rise to diverging special theories falling under the one generic position.

Both the Natural Right and the Social Good theories disagree with this analysis, and they offer definitions of a fundamentally different kind. While agreeing that justice is complex, they claim that the source of the complexity lies in the objective meaning of justice itself, and not in the fact that it may also have further subjective meanings. Hence, in seeking to define justice, they, in effect, analyze a complex notion into its fundamental parts. The definition is analytic in the sense of identifying the most important element entering into the composition—*i.e.*, that element which will serve to illuminate the most important uses of justice. Disagreement arises over the identity of this element. One theory bases its account of justice on the notion of the social good or the social utility, whereas the other theory appeals to the notion of natural right.

Positive Law and Social Good writers disagree about the definition of justice, but both agree that the ancient Roman definition does not adequately define its meaning. They hold that what is one's own or one's right cannot be the basic element, since this itself depends upon another notion—upon law, according to the one theory, upon the social good, according to the other. Only the Natural Right theory accepts the adequacy of the Roman definition, as it stands, and it does so by taking what is one's own, right, or due, as grounded ultimately on man's nature.

The Natural Right theory is the most complex of the three. At the root of this complexity is the notion of natural right itself. It has a different status within the controversy from that of the other two privileged terms. None of the theories denies the meaningfulness of either "law" or "social good," although each theory has its own interpretation of them. But two of the theories deny the very existence of such a thing as natural right, and, hence, they deny the meaningfulness of the term. Of course, both the Positive Law theory and the Social Good theory admit that justice has something to do with rights, but they deny that there is any natural right. Thus, verbally and conceptually, "natural right" does not appear in the account of justice offered by two of the theories, except as an object of denial, whereas it is the basic and privileged term of the Natural Right theory.

This theory asserts that natural right is necessary for understanding the full meaning of justice. It can admit that justice may sometimes consist in doing what conforms to the law or serves the common good, but it insists that this is so only if neither case violates natural right. For this theory, law and the social good are conditions of justice only as understood, at least implicitly, in relation to natural right. Thus the privileged terms of the other two theories are included within the Natural Right account of justice, although on its own interpretation of their relation to justice.

The fact that the Natural Right theory has the greatest number of variants furnishes another sign that it is the most complex of the three theories. There are more points at which men can disagree. The differences also seem to go deeper. This is perhaps most apparent from the split arising from the notion of a social contract. There are proponents of each theory who find this notion useful for the analysis of justice, and there are some who do not. Thus, with regard to this feature, Hobbes stands opposed to Kelsen within the Positive Law theory, Mill to Rawls within the Social Good theory, and Locke to Aquinas within the Natural Right theory. But the split seems widest and deepest in the last case. Natural right for Locke seems to rest exclusively on the individual, and amounts to an immunity that the individual should have from the claims and interference of society. But for Aquinas, at least as interpreted by many of his followers, natural right rests on the social nature of man, and the rights of society as well as of the individual are equally natural.

There are many other variations of the one general Natural Right theory, arising from different interpretations of natural right. As we have seen, some hold that there is only one natural right, others that there are many rights that can be explicitly enunciated, while still others hold that no precise determination is possible. Although all proponents agree that natural right can be known, they differ widely about the way in which it is known. Some hold that natural rights are self-evident and can be rationally grasped by anyone whose natural reason is not perverted. Others hold that they are grasped by intuition or by some sort of sense or feeling. Some hold that the knowledge of natural right is socially conditioned and dependent upon men's social experience, whereas others assert that it is independent of society. All agree that there is a natural obligation to do what is naturally just, but much disagreement arises when it comes to explaining the source of this obligation.

The differences among the proponents of the theory are admittedly great, greater than those among the variants in either of the other two theories. Yet all agree that natural right somehow provides a basis for justice, and that neither law nor the social good suffices to account for the most important meanings of justice.

The Social Good theory remains, as it were, in the middle, sharing some points with each of the other two theories. With the Positive Law theory it shares the position that justice is not based on natural right, since rights are held to depend on society and social recognition. With the Natural Right theory, it maintains that justice is a wider notion than law, so that justice cannot be identified with legality. A sign of the fact that the Social Good theory occupies a mid-position appears in the way the subspecies of the theory tend to approach the positions taken by one or the other of the two remaining theories. Some adherents of the theory, like Hume, come close to the Positive Law position, whereas others, like Sidgwick, approach much closer to the Natural Right position.

That the Positive Law theory and the Natural Right theory are extremes is evident from the fact that, once an author adopts the positions characteristic of one of the two theories, there is no doubt that he is opposed to the positions of the other. The denial that justice rests on natural right combined with the assertion that it is identical with legality, understood as that of the positive law, establishes a position unequivocally opposed to that which asserts the first and denies the second proposition. And that is precisely the situation between the two theories.

The relative complexity of the three theories can be manifested by displaying in summary fashion how each theory would interpret justice with reference to its common notes and the three privileged terms. All three agree that justice obliges us to do something that is good and that concerns another. Spelling out what it obliges us to do, we obtain the following:

(1) It obliges us to obey the law.
(2) It obliges us to do what promotes the social good.
(3) It obliges us to render to each what belongs to him as a natural right.

The Natural Right theory is the most complex of the three theories because it alone asserts all three propositions. The third, of course, is the controlling one, since it is implicit in both the first and second in the sense that it asserts them only on the understanding that neither violates natural right.

The Social Good theory asserts the first and second but denies the third, claiming as it does that there is no such thing as a natural right. Implicitly, it also claims that the first proposition depends upon the second, since the justice of a law is held to depend on its serving for the social good.

The Positive Law theory is the simplest in that it asserts only the first proposition: Justice obliges us to obey the law, but not to promote the common good or render another his natural right as something that could be separate and distinct from obeying the law.

THE NUMBER OF THE BASIC THEORIES

Further understanding of the shape of the controversy as well as of the complexity of the theories can be gained by considering why there are only three basic theories.

We have seen, in determining the subject of the controversy, that for all the theories with which we have been concerned, justice is a social norm. This is to say that it provides rules by which men ought to regulate their conduct in associating with one another. Justice, then, is a relational concept in that it involves more than one term— that is, it supposes many men.

The fact that justice is a relation provides in itself the basis for two different approaches to the analysis of justice. One may concentrate on and emphasize the relation itself, that is, that aspect in which many are associated together. Or one may concentrate on and emphasize, not the relation but the terms that enter into it, the entities that are encompassed by the relation.

This difference in approach or consideration provides a means of distinguishing the basic theories of justice. One group, consisting of the Positive Law and Social Good theories, places the norm of justice in the relationship itself, in the fact that there is an association in which men lead a common life and which has certain requirements of its own. The other position, taken by the Natural Right theory, places it basically, not in the relationship but in the terms entering it, the fact that it is men that are engaged in joint activities.

It would be neat and clear if the difference between the theories were simply that one position locates the basis of justice in society while the other locates it in the individual. But matters are not this simple. There are authors in the Natural Right position who argue as though the difference were only this much and claim that what is due to man as a natural right is his as an individual. But, against this, other authors criticize such individualism and claim that natural right is rooted in man as a social being. Where both agree, however, is in the claim that human rights are not conferred exclusively and entirely by society and social recognition. Men can demand as their right what is needed for their own development and perfection and not because it is something that is good for society, even though it may be obtained only in and through society. It is argued, for example, that parents have a right to respect and children a right to education, not because the recognition of such rights is needed for the good of the family or because there are positive laws to enforce them but because of what it is to be a parent or a child.

This first distinction regarding the basis of justice as a social norm thus yields a division in which the Natural Right position falls on one side by maintaining that the basis is to be found in the terms of the relation, while both the Positive Law and the Social Good theories fall on the other side by holding that the basis lies in the relationship itself.

The notion of justice as a social relation yields still another way of distinguishing the two latter theories from each other. One may regard any social relation primarily in view of either the intrinsic or the extrinsic factors that bring it about and hold it together. The Social Good theory follows the second approach and holds that the end is the overriding feature of the social relationship; it is what men want to achieve by associating together, and the conditions for their associating, that determine what must be done and what the laws should be. The Positive Good position denies that the end, the social good, is definite enough to supply an objective social norm and affirms, instead, that the norm is intrinsic to any society in the rules by which men govern themselves, that is to say, in the positive law of the society. The basic difference between these two positions lies in the way the norm is conceived and the objectivity and definiteness that is demanded of it, and not in whether it rests primarily on the relationship rather than on its terms.

From the way of viewing the controversy, it appears that the most fundamental of all the differences between the theories concerns the understanding of the relation between justice and society. For all, justice is a social virtue and a norm governing man's conduct toward others. But one group of theories holds that it is based exclusively on society and ordered to the good of society or its laws, whereas the other group maintains that it is ultimately based on what man is, and not exclusively on his society.

This difference is manifest in the interpretations given of the classical definition of justice as rendering to each his due. The one position claims that there is something that is due to man as man, while the other denies this and declares that what is due is meaningless until it receives determination within society in terms of its aims or laws.

The accounts offered by the various theories of the approbative and obligatory character of justice reveal the same fundamental difference. For one position, the just thing to do elicits approval and imposes an obligation basically because it is seen to be a just, that is, a good that ought to be done. For the other position, both the approbation and the obligatoriness belonging to justice stem ultimately from society or from its laws. Except for the good of others or that of the association of which he is a member, man has no reason to approve of justice, no obligation to conform his actions to its norm. The just thing is not something that a man can claim as his by right as belonging to his perfection, nor is it what he owes another because he is a man. In fact, for the one position, shared by both the Soical Good and the Positive Law theories, justice frequently is pictured as a compromise between what men would like to have and what they can actually obtain through their association with others; it is not a good in and for itself, as it is for the other position.

The differing conceptions of the relation between justice and society appear also in the accounts that are given of justice as a virtue. For all, it is a social virtue—an excellence of character in man's conduct toward others. But in the one case, the emphasis is so heavily upon justice as a good and a virtue that is good in itself that justice is in danger of being confused with the moral good as such. According to the other theories, justice is identified with obedience or assimilated to benevolence, but in either case it is subordinated to the good of others and that of the whole association. In this case the virtue of justice is inculcated and held up as a need of society: If men cease to do the just thing, their society itself will be jeopardized. In the case of the other position, doing injustice to another is to wrong him as a man, to do harm to oneself and, thence, only in consequence, to harm also the mutual association.

The difference here is largely one of emphasis, since, as noted, for all the theories, justice is a social virtue. Yet, the difference is a real one—according as the place of primacy is given to the social relationship and the good of others or to man and his rights as they enter into this relationship. What is at issue is the priority of man or society in accounting for justice. Is it what man is and his good that supplies the basic rule of justice, or does this derive rather from what society is and its good? In this formulation of the basic difference, man need not, in fact he should not, be taken as an individual somehow set against society. In both cases, he is to be understood as man existing in society, educated in it, and, for a large part, formed by it. Justice, likewise, is granted to be a social norm and its achievement a social good. Once all these qualifications are made, the questions can still be asked, whether justice so conceived is rooted ultimately in man and his rights as man or in society, its needs and goods. Some theories give logical priority to society in the account they give of justice; others give it to man and his rights.

If the fundamental difference between the theories is as stated, the issue over natural right is the crucial one, since it divides all theories into two groups according as natural right is affirmed or denied. On this score, the Positive Law theory should be more closely related to the Social Good theory than either is to the Natural Right account of justice.

Yet this feature by itself is not sufficient to support the claim that the controversy over justice should be viewed as essentially two-sided. Although the issues over law and objectivity, taken singly, are not so important in their pervasive influence as the issue over natural right, they are so when taken together. For, then, they serve to draw a distinct separation between the Positive Law and Social Good theories. What is more, they do so in such a way as to involve also the Natural Right theory, with the result that the Social Good theory appears, as it were, in the middle, between the other two theories as extremes.

Needless to say, there is no implication that the middle position on this analysis is a golden mean and the best and truest version of justice. All that this indicates is that the controversy over justice is more accurately described as three-sided.

It is three-sided, not only because there are three sides but also because there are three main issues, which are posed respectively by the privileged term characterizing each of the three theories. As we have seen, there are two issues on which two of the theories join in common opposition against the third. On the issue of the relation between justice and law, the proponents of the Social Good and the Natural Right theories share a common cause against the identification of objective justice with legality asserted by the Positive Law theory. But, on the issue of the relation between justice and natural right, the Social Good theory agrees with the Positive Law theory in denying natural right. With respect to these two issues, the controversy is clearly characterized by two theories opposing a third.

The issue of the relation between justice and the social good manifests a different pattern. On this issue the Natural Right theory shares something with both the Positive Law and the Social Good theories. It agrees with the Positive Law theory in denying that justice is ultimately based on promoting the social good, but it refuses to go along with this latter theory in holding that the social good can never afford a basis for objective justice. The Natural Right theory agrees with the Social Good theory that the just thing may sometimes consist in preserving and promoting the common good; it denies only that the social good is, to the exclusion of natural right, the entire basis of justice.

The controversy concerning justice contains, as it were, three subcontroversies: one over legality, another over natural right, and a third over the social good. To bring the three theories into confrontation with one another we must consider the arguments each advances in support of its own position and against its opponents. To that task we now turn. In order to delineate as sharply as I can the three-sided controversy, I will endeavor to state as clearly and briefly as possible only the major arguments. I will also forgo providing any further documentation, and rely entirely on what has been given in the previous chapters. In this, my aim is to provide a simplified and clear summary of the entire controversy.

THE CONTROVERSY OVER LEGALITY

The Positive Law position about justice consists essentially in two points: First, the assertion that justice is identical with legality, and, second, the claim that justice used in any other sense either reduces to legality or else is without a determinate and objective meaning. In opposition to these claims, the other two basic theories take the position that justice is a wider notion than legality, and that, when it is used in these other wider senses, it still has an objective and determinate meaning.

The argument for justice being wider than law consists essentially of two points. One is the claim that justice is appealed to in matters where there is no positive law and where there should be none. The other point is that justice itself supplies a criterion of law and, hence, cannot be identical with legality, since no law can provide a measure of itself.

The counterargument of the Positive Law theory is more complex. It passes beyond the immediate issue of legality to that of objectivity and the question of what is to count as an objective and determinate norm of human action. All theories accept as a common datum of the controversy that justice is a norm of social action. Differences arise then, not over whether or not justice is a norm, but over what provides the basis of the norm and what characteristics a norm should have.

All three theories, although each in its own way, grant that law can provide a norm of justice. The Positive Law theory goes on to claim that law alone provides a basic norm that is determinate and objective. The position as such need not deny that people do sometimes use justice to mean something more than legality. It does deny, however, that when so used it has any definite and objective meaning. If justice is taken to be a criterion of law itself, a measure of its goodness, justice is obviously being used to mean more than merely legality. Otherwise, to say that a law is just is to say only that it is legal. There is no doubt that justice is commonly appealed to as the ground for making more serious judgments of the law than this. The Positive Law theory need not deny that this is the case. Again, it maintains only that such judgments lack definiteness and objectivity. The controversy between the Positive Law theory, on the one side, and both the Social Good and the Natural Right theories, on the other, thus involves the further issue of the objectivity of justice.

Why does one theory assert that only positive law provides an objective and determinate norm of justice, while the other two theories deny this claim? The source and ground of the disagreements become clearer from considering how it can be maintained that natural right provides an objective norm of justice, since the arguments for and against natural right concern in large part the same questions about norms that are involved in the issues about legality.

THE CONTROVERSY OVER NATURAL RIGHT

The basic and minimal position common to all adherents of the Natural Right theory consists in the claim that natural right is the basis of justice. This is to be understood as asserting that it is possible to conceive what is due man as his right by considering his nature. Nature in some way provides the ultimate criterion of justice, a basic norm of how men should act toward one another. It is a norm common to all men and a standard to govern their acts, not only in organized political society with its law, but also within the family, and even in any chance encounter men might have with others outside the bounds of society.

That there is a natural norm of justice is claimed by all proponents of the theory: Man has natural rights, that is to say, rights that are not conferred by society but that belong to him merely because he is a man. But there is wide difference of opinion regarding the way they come to be known. Some Natural Right authors hold that man would know them even if he lived entirely outside society. But others maintain that men ordinarily learn about their rights through the laws of society. What is essential to the position is not agreement on how men come to learn about their natural rights, but that such rights exist. For if there are such rights, then there is a basis for maintaining that an act may be just because it is according to nature and not because it is prescribed by law or needed for the good of society. Man can justly claim what is necessary to him for his existence as a man.

The main arguments against this position reduce to three, all of which are common to both the Positive Law and the Social Good theories of justice. They may be summarily described as the argument from variability, from indefiniteness, and from the mode of justification.

The argument from variability rests on the claim that there is no general, unchanging agreement to be found among men regarding the content of natural right. What is declared to be a natural right in one society is denied in another, or the same society will both affirm and deny it at different times, or within the same society at any one time some will assert as a natural right what others deny. Slavery provides the classic example. Only a few generations ago, Christians of one and the same society were bitterly and deeply divided over whether it was naturally unjust to hold a person in chattel slavery. So, too, there was a time when many men, including theologians, philosophers, and lawyers, denied that slavery is naturally unjust, whereas those who today assert the existence of natural right would almost unanimously hold that it is unjust, even though chattel slavery may still continue to exist in some parts of the world.

Given the fact of such variability, the opponents maintain that there can be no such thing as natural right, since, if there were, it would have to be invariable and immutable.

Against this argument, the Natural Right theory advances a two-part answer. On the one hand, it denies that the variation and disagreement are as great as is charged. On the other hand, it offers an explanation of why disagreement should be expected with regard to natural right.

On the first point, it is claimed that agreement and invariability are to be found among all men in all cultures and all times regarding certain principles of social conduct, based on such convictions as the following: that taking a human life differs in seriousness from taking any other kind of life; that sexual relations need some regulation; that men need rules and prohibitions to lead a common life. The fact that different rules in custom and law have been elaborated by different societies is no argument, it is maintained, against the general agreement about such convictions as these.

Again, it is argued that, even if variability about natural right and principles of justice were as great as maintained, this, by itself, would not prove that the principles of right are variable. It would show only that men have different notions of justice. Opinions can vary without the object of the opinion itself varying. The earth has only one shape, for example, but men have had different opinions about what that shape is.

Disagreement about natural right thus is asserted to be understandable. Natural right is not something that is known in the same way as the sensible qualities of a physical object. The injustice of one man killing another is not a quality like the redness of Cain's hair. Knowledge of natural right is held by its proponents to be sometimes difficult to acquire. In complex cases, it may be hard to know, but this difficulty, it is claimed, is no argument against its existence, any more than the difficulty of deciding a law case is any argument against the existence of the law.

Still further reasons for disagreement are taken from the way natural right is held to be known. But these are more appropriate to consideration of the argument about justification.

The argument from indefiniteness holds that natural right is too vague to provide a norm for human conduct. Justice, it is argued, must be a precise standard; a just man is one who is exact and precise in his conduct. Yet, definiteness and precision are the very features that are lacking, it is claimed, in natural right. The principle that equals should be treated equally is often cited as an example of a natural right. But this principle, it is argued, is so indefinite as to be empty and meaningless, since by itself it does not contain any criterion of applicability. It does not specify the respects in which equality is to be observed. People may be equal or unequal in many different respects: in height, weight, age, strength, health, virtue, knowledge, language, earning power, savings, possessions, citizenship, playing billiards, golf, poker, etc., athletic ability, fighting ability, brain power, virility, drinking or eating capacity, and many, many other respects. But which of these are to be taken as relevant for applying the principle that equals should be treated equally? The principle does not say. For this reason it is held to be useless as a norm of justice.

The proponents of the Natural Right position admit the charge of indefiniteness and yet deny that this constitutes an argument against its existence or standing as a norm. Natural right, it is argued, may be expressed, first, in such general tendencies as those cited above, which come to be specified and determined in definite rules only through the experience of men living together. Natural right, in this sense, provides only the principle. It is through living and working out solutions for the problems of his daily life that man comes to discover how the principle is to be applied and realized. Laws and social practices thus may be held to be special applications and determinations of natural right.

Proponents of natural right admit that progress may occur in the knowledge of natural right. Through historical development, men come to see more clearly what belongs to natural right. It is maintained, for example, that men see more clearly today than ever before the injustice of chattel slavery and the justice of women's rights. Men also come to learn what equalities and inequalities are relevant to observance of the principle that equals should be treated equally. But the principle itself is held to be given, as it were, by nature—that is to say, it is not a convention made by law or a practice decided upon for the good of society.

The third general argument, that which concerns the justification of natural right, underlies both the preceding arguments from variability and from indefiniteness. It is also a point on which the Positive Law and Social Good theories begin to diverge. Up to this point, they have been joined in common acceptance of the arguments denying the existence of natural right. Both also hold that the theory is weak in its account of the way in which natural right is known and justified, but they do so, finally, for different reasons.

Both, to begin with, agree in arguing that natural right is without rational justification since it has no objective basis and is not known in a way that can be verified or confirmed by any disinterested observer. Natural right, it is claimed, seems to be more a matter of faith than of evidence, and the appeal to intuition and to self-evidence used by its proponents is dismissed as a repudiation of reason and as a confession of ignorance. The notion of natural right as an indemonstrable first principle is rejected as irrational.

Although both the Positive Law and the Social Good theories would advance this claim, they would do so for different reasons. The Positive Law position denies the objectivity of all moral or value judgments and, hence, the rationality of natural right as a moral principle. The Social Good position refuses to go so far as to deny the objectivity of all moral judgments, but it does maintain that only society can provide a social norm such as justice.

This is the point at which the controversy may be said to come to a standstill. Up to now, we have been faced with issues on which arguments can be given pro and con. But we have now come to what seems to be more like a question of fact, but a fact of which fundamentally discordant accounts are given. The Natural Right position maintains, in effect, that one need only see what man is as man to recognize that he has a right to life; that is, that his life has to be respected in a way fundamentally different from that of other living things, and that it cannot be taken justly without serious reasons in justification. Against this claim, the other two theories maintain that they see no such thing; there is no natural right to life; there is only the right that men have come to recognize as a result of legal or social achievement.

The difficulty at this point derives in large part from the difficulty of ascertaining how an answer can be found to the question being asked. All three theories admit, for example, that man has a right to life. The question then arises—Why does he have a right to life? What is its basis? The one theory appeals to natural right, while the other two refuse to admit such an appeal.

Between these two answers, what way is there to decide? Men now obviously learn of their rights through living and being educated in society. For this reason, Natural Right authors frequently invent imaginary cases of how primitive men might have acquired knowledge of right, or they imagine as a kind of ideal experiment what man would be like living outside the bounds of society, and how he would act. Such examples are dismissed by their opponents as "Desert Island" cases of very questionable value in themselves and without any force as evidence. At this point in the controversy, we face the fundamental question of what is to count as moral reasoning and good evidence in deciding questions of value. The Positive Law theory tends to take the position that there is no such thing, since moral judgment is held to be finally entirely a question of personal choice and of subjective feeling. The Social Good theory holds that moral judgments have an objective basis, but that this basis is provided, not by the nature of man but by what is needed for men to live together to achieve their social good.

The Controversy over the Social Good

Further light on the complexity of the controversy over the norm of justice and its objectivity can be gained from considering the objections brought against the Social Good theory by the other two theories. As already noted, the controversy changes its shape when viewed from this aspect. In the case of either one of the other two positions, the two opponents share a common opposition to the third and, for the most part, can appeal to the same arguments. Against the identification of justice with legality, the Social Good and the Natural Right theories can argue from the same evidence to show that justice is a wider notion and applies to conditions in which any question of law is irrelevant. So, too, against the existence of natural right, the Social Good theory can appeal for the most part to the same arguments that are used by the Positive Law theory. There is no such common ground, however, underlying the opposition of the Positive Law and the Natural Right theories to the Social Good position. Both are opposed, but for fundamentally different reasons.

The Positive Law theory maintains that the social good is no better than natural right for providing an objective norm of justice. Until it is definitely settled by the members of a society, the good or utility of society is indeterminate. Worse than that, it is also an object of dispute, since men in good conscience can disagree about what is best for their society to pursue. Not only is there disagreement about it but both individuals and societies change their opinions about the social good. It thus lacks the first essentials of a norm of justice, namely, that of furnishing an invariable, determinate, and objective standard by which men can determine questions of justice and injustice in their social conduct. According to the Positive Law theory, no such standard exists until men have established the laws by which they wish to govern themselves. In doing this, they define the social good in the sense that they establish the goals of their society that they will pursue in common, along with the rights and duties needed as means for its achievement. Apart from positive law, it is claimed that social good is no less chimerical than natural right as a norm of justice.

The Natural Right theory will have none of this argument. It would side with the Social Good theory in maintaining that the good of society does sometimes, in fact, serve as an objective principle of justice. Against this theory, it argues only that the social good is not the only and principal basis of justice. It denies that the rules of justice are entirely and exclusively the result of man's efforts to achieve a good social life. The need for justice does not derive entirely from the need to achieve the good of others. Justice is a matter of right that ultimately belongs to every man for his own self-perfection. Justice is not always a question of the good of others or the good of the greatest number, or even the good of society. It is no accident that the declarations of the rights of man were first made by appeal to natural right, nor that the argument for this position is often made by appealing to man imagined as living apart from any organized society, with common practices and laws.

The counterarguments of the Social Good theory vary, of course, with the opponent. Yet, against neither of them does it have any argument that is characteristically its own. It shares the support of the Natural Right position in maintaining that human social life lays down certain conditions that have to be met to achieve a minimal common good. Men are vulnerable, hence, there has to be some forbearance of violence. Insofar as they are approximately equal, they will have to compromise and exercise mutual forbearance. Their unselfishness, resources, and understanding are all severely limited, hence, it is necessary to lay down rules and sanctions to govern their actions. All these conditions, it is held, establish so many general norms or directions that must be observed by the laws established in society. They provide a basis for justice as a criterion of the law itself. The social good understood in this way as what is needed for achieving a good human society is held to provide a basis of justice over and above that of the positive law.

Against the Natural Right position, the Social Good theory joins forces with the Positive Law theory in maintaining that justice is exclusively the result of society. Without the effort to lead a common life, men would have no need for justice, and if one could conceive of men living apart from society, there would be no justice, nor any morality at all. If "conventional" is taken to mean no more than the negation of natural right as defined above, then the Social Good position is no less conventional than that of the Positive Law theory.

With this we have completed our summary of the major arguments in the three-sided controversy about justice. We have also completed the task that we set for ourselves in the beginning. We have provided a dialectical clarification of the idea of justice. In this endeavor, which has involved surveying and analyzing a vast literature, we have pursued one ideal throughout: to achieve that degree of certitude that the subject matter admits, and to see more clearly than has yet been seen the shape of the controversy concerning justice.

Bibliography

Ahrens, H. *Cours de Droit Naturel.* Leipzig: F. A. Brockhaus, 1892.

Allen, C. K. *Aspects of Justice.* London: Stevens, 1958.

————. *Law in the Making.* London: Oxford University Press, 1961.

Aquinas, St. Thomas. *In Decem Libros Ethicorum Aristotelis ad Nicomachum Expositio,* ed. A. M. Pirotta. Turin: Marietti, 1934.

————. *Summa Theologica.* Ottawa: Commisio Piana, 1963.

Aristotle. *The Nicomachean Ethics,* ed. H. Rackham. London: W. Heinemann, 1934.

————. *The Politics,* ed. H. Rackham. London: W. Heinemann, 1932.

Audisio, G. *Juris Naturae et Gentium Privati et Publici Fundamenti.* Rome: De Propaganda Fide, 1852.

Augustine, St. *The City of God,* ed. W. C. Greene. Cambridge, Mass.: Harvard University Press, 1960.

Austin, J. *The Province of Jurisprudence Determined,* ed. H. L. A. Hart. London: Weidenfeld & Nicolson, 1954.

Baier, K. *The Moral Point of View.* New York: Random House, 1965.

Barry, B. M. "Justice and the Common Good," *Analysis,* 31 (1961), 86–90.

Baumol, W. J. *Welfare Economics and the Theory of the State.* Cambridge, Mass.: Harvard University Press, 1965.

Baylis, C. A. *Ethics.* New York: Holt, Rinehart & Winston, 1958.

Becker, C. L. *The Declaration of Independence.* New York: Vintage Books, 1958.

Becker, W. G. "Gerechtigkeit," *Revue internationale de philosophie,* 41 (1957), 363–391.

Benn, S. I. and Peters, R. S. *Social Principle and the Democratic State.* London: Allen & Unwin, 1959.

Bentham, J. *An Introduction to the Principles of Morals and Legislation,* ed. L. J. Lafleur. New York: Hafner, 1961.

————. *Bentham's Theory of Fiction,* ed. C. K. Ogden. Paterson, N.J.: Littlefield Adams & Co., 1959.

Biavaschi, G. B. *Il diretto naturale.* Udine: Arti Grafiche friulane, 1953.

Bienenfeld, F. R. *Rediscovery of Justice.* London: Allen & Unwin, 1947.

Blackstone, W. *Commentaries on the Laws of England.* Philadelphia: J. B. Lippincott, 1872.

181

Blanchard, B. "The Objectivity of Moral Judgment," *Revue internationale de philosophie,* 70 (1964), 361–378.
———. *Reason and Goodness.* London: Allen & Unwin, 1961.
Bobbio, N. "Sul Positivismo Giuridico," *Rivista di filosofia,* 52 (1961), 14–34.
Boulding, K. E. "Social Justice in Social Dynamics," in Brandt, *Social Justice,* pp. 73–92.
Braithwaite, R. B. *Theory of Games as a Tool for the Moral Philosopher.* London: Cambridge University Press, 1963.
Brandt, R. B. *Ethical Theory.* Englewood Cliffs, N.J. Prentice-Hall, 1959.
——— (ed.). *Social Justice.* Englewood Cliffs, N.J. Prentice-Hall, 1962.
Brecht, A. "The Ultimate Standard of Justice," *Nomos VI,* pp. 62–68.
Brentano, Fr. *The Origin of the Knowledge of Right and Wrong.* Translated by C. Hague. London: A. Constable, 1902.
Broad, C. D. *Five Types of Ethical Theory.* London: Routledge & Kegan Paul, 1962.
———. "On the Functions of False Hypotheses in Ethics," *International Journal of Ethics,* 26 (1916), 377–397.
Brown, S. M. "Inalienable Rights," *Philosophical Review,* 64 (1955), 192–211.
Brunner, H. E. *Justice and The Social Order.* Translated by M. Hottinger. New York: Harper & Bros., 1945.
Bryce, J. *Studies in History and Jurisprudence.* New York and London: Oxford University Press, 1901.
Burlamaqui, J. *Principles of Natural and Politic Law.* Columbus, Ohio: J. H. Riley, 1857.
Cahn, E. N. *The Sense of Injustice.* New York: New York University Press, 1949.
Cicero. *De finibus,* ed. C. F. W. Muller. Leipzig: B. G. Teubner, 1908.
———. *De inventione,* ed. Friedrich. Leipzig: B. G. Teubner, 1884.
———. *De officiis,* ed. C. Atzert. Leipzig: B. G. Teubner, 1923.
———. *De Republica,* ed. K. Ziegler. Leipzig: B. G. Teubner, 1929.
Civardi, L. *Christianity and Social Justice.* Translated by S. Andriano. Fresno, Calif.: Academy Guild Press, 1961.
Cogley, J. (ed.). *Natural Law and Modern Society.* Cleveland, Ohio: World Publishing, 1963.
Cohen, F. S. *Ethical Systems and Legal Ideals.* Ithaca, N.Y.: Cornell University Press, 1959.
Corkey, R. "Benevolence and Justice," *Philosophical Quarterly,* 9 (1959), 152–163.
Croce, B. *Libertà et Giustizia.* Bari, 1944.
Del Vecchio, G. *La Giustizia.* 6th ed. Rome: Editrice Studium, 1959.
———. *Justice. An Historical and Philosophical Essay,* ed. A. H. Campbell. Edinburgh: Edinburgh University Press, 1956.
De Rooy, P. E. *Lectiones Philosophiae socialis: Pars generalis.* Rome: Angelicum, 1936–37.
Dowrick, E. *Justice according to the English Common Lawyers.* London: Butterworth, 1961.
Drago, G. *La Giustizia e le Giustizie.* Milan: Mazorati Editore, 1963.
Le droit naturel, in *Institut International de Philosophie Politique: Annales III.* Paris: Presses universitaires, 1959.
Dupréel, E. *Traité de morale.* Brussels, 1932.

Ellul, J, *Le Fondement théologique du droit.* Paris: Delachaux & Niestlé, 1946.
Emmet, D. *Justice and the Law.* London: Lindsay Press, 1963.
Ewing, A. S. *Ethics.* London: English Universities Press, 1960.
Feinberg, J. "Justice and Personal Desert," *Nomos VI,* pp. 69–97.
Ferree, W. *The Act of Social Justice.* Washington, D.C.: Catholic University of America Press, 1942.
Fichte, J. G. *Grundlage des Naturrechts.* Leipzig: F. Meiner, 1922.
Foscolo, U. *Sull' origine e i limiti della giustizia.* 1809.
Frankena, W. K. "The Concept of Social Justice," in Brandt, *Social Justice,* pp. 1–29.
———. "Natural and Inalienable Rights," *Philosophical Review,* 64 (1955), 212–232.
Freund, P. A. "Social Justice and The Law," in Brandt, *Social Justice,* pp. 93–117.
Fried, C. "Justice and Liberty," *Nomos VI,* pp. 126–146.
———. "Natural Law and the Concept of Justice," *Ethics,* 74 (1964), 237–254.
Friedrich, C. J. "Justice: the Just Political Act," *Nomos VI,* pp. 24–43.
———. *The Philosophy of Law in Historical Perspective.* Chicago: University of Chicago Press, 1963.
———. *Transcendent Justice: The Religious Dimension of Constitutionalism.* Durham: Duke University Press, 1964.
Fuller, L. *The Morality of Law.* New Haven: Yale University Press, 1964.
Gareis, K. *Vom Begriff Gerechtigkeit.* Giessen, 1907.
Garlan, E. N. *Legal Realism and Justice.* New York: Columbia University Press, 1941.
Garin, E. "Giustizia," *Revue internationale de philosphie,* 41 (1957), 268–301.
Gewirth, A. "Meanings and Criteria in Ethics," *Philosophy,* 38 (1963), 329–345.
———. "Political Justice," in Brandt, *Social Justice,* pp. 119–169.
Gillet, M. *Conscience chretienne et justice sociale.* Paris: Revue des Jeunes, 1922.
Ginsberg, M. *On Justice in Society.* Ithaca, N.Y.: Cornell University Press, 1965.
Godwin, W. *Enquiry concerning Political Justice and its Influence on Morals and Happiness.* Toronto: Toronto University Press, 1946.
Green, T. H. *Lectures on the Principles of Political Obligation.* London: Longmans, Green & Co., 1950.
Grotius, H. *De iure belli et pacis.* Washington, D.C.: Carnegie Institution, 1925.
Gurvitch, G. *L'expérience juridique et la philosophie pluraliste du droit.* Paris: A. Pedone, 1935.
———. *L'idée du droit social.* Paris: Librarie Sirey, 1932.
———. "Justice," in *Encyclopedia of the Social Sciences,* Vol. 4, pp. 509–514.
Hare, R. M. *The Language of Morals.* Oxford: Clarendon Press, 1961.
———. *Freedom and Reason.* Oxford: Clarendon Press, 1963.
Harrison, J. "Utilitarianism, Universalization, and Our Duty to be Just," in Olafson (ed.), *Justice and Social Policy,* pp. 55–79.

Hart, H. L. A. "Are There any Natural Rights," *Philosophical Review,* 64 (1955), 175–191.

————. *The Concept of Law.* Oxford: Clarendon Press, 1961.

Hayek, F. A. *Road to Serfdom.* Chicago: University of Chicago Press, 1950.

Hegel, G. W. F. *Philosophy of Right.* Translated by T. M. Knox. Oxford: Clarendon Press, 1945.

Hobbes, T. *The Leviathan.* Oxford: Clarendon Press, 1947.

Hobhouse, L. T. *The Elements of Social Justice.* London: Allen & Unwin, 1949.

————. *Morals in Evolution.* London: Chapman & Hall, 1951.

Hocking, W. E. "Justice, Law and the Cases," in Sayre, *Interpretations,* pp. 332 ff.

————. *Present Status of the Philosophy of Law and Rights.* New Haven: Yale University Press, 1926.

Hohfeld, W. N. *Fundamental Legal Conceptions as applied in Judicial Reasoning and other Legal Essays.* New Haven: Yale University Press, 1923.

Holmes, O. W. *Holmes-Laski Letters.* Cambridge, Mass.: Harvard University Press, 1953.

Hook, S. (ed.). *Law and Philosophy: A Symposium.* New York: New York University Press, 1964.

Hooker, R. *Of the Laws of Ecclesiastical Polity.* Oxford: Oxford University Press, 1888.

————. "A Learned Sermon on the Nature of Pride," in *Works,* Vol. 2, pp. 696–738, Oxford: Oxford University Press, 1888.

Hospers, J. *Human Conduct.* New York: Harcourt, Brace & World, 1961.

Hume, D. *An Enquiry concerning the Principles of Morals,* ed. L. A. Selby-Bigge. Oxford: Clarendon Press, 1894.

————. *A Treatise of Human Nature,* ed. L. A. Selby-Bigge. Oxford: Clarendon Press, 1955.

Ihering, R. *L'évolution du droit* (*Zweck im Recht*). Paris: Chevalier-Marescq, 1901.

Institutionum et regularum iuris Romani Syntagina, ed. R. Gneist. Leipzig: B. G. Teubner, 1880.

Jefferson, T. *Writings.* Washington, D.C.: Thomas Jefferson Memorial Association, 1905.

Justinian. *Imperatoris Iustiniani Institutionum,* ed. J. B. Moyle. Oxford: Oxford University Press, 1883.

Kant, I. "General Introduction to the Metaphysic of Morals," in *Great Books of the Western World.* Chicago: Encyclopaedia Britannica Inc., 1952. Vol. 42.

————. "The Science of Right," in *Great Books of the Western World.* Chicago: Encyclopaedia Britannica Inc., 1952. Vol. 42.

Kelsen, H. *General Theory of Law and State.* New York: Russell & Russell, 1961.

————. "Justice et droit naturel," in *Le droit naturel,* pp. 1–123.

————. "The Metamorphoses of The Idea of Justice," in Sayre, *Interpretations,* pp. 390–418.

————. *What is Justice?.* Berkeley: University of California Press, 1957.

Knight, F. H. "On the Meaning of Justice," *Nomos VI,* pp. 1–23.

Lafargue, P. "The Origin of the Idea of Justice," in *Social and Political Studies.* Chicago: University of Chicago Press, 1906.

Laslett, P. (ed.). *Philosophy, Politics and Society.* New York: Macmillan Publishing Co., 1956.

Leclercq, J. *Les droits et devoirs individuels.* Namur: Wesmael-Charlier, 1946.

————. *Le fundement de droit et de la société.* Namur: Wesmael-Charlier, 1947.

————. *Leçons de droit naturel.* Namur: Wesmael-Charlier, 1948.

Leibniz, G. W. "On the Notions of Right and Justice," in *Philosophical Papers and Letters,* ed. L. E. Loemker. Chicago: University of Chicago Press, 1956.

————. *Scritti politici e di diritto naturale.* Turin, 1951.

Lloyd, D. *The Idea of Law.* Baltimore: Penguin Books, 1964.

Locke, J. *Essays on The Law of Nature.* ed. W. von Leyden. Oxford: Clarendon Press, 1958.

————. *Two Treatises of Civil Government.* New York: E. P. Dutton & Co., 1943.

Lugo, J. de. *Disputatio de Justitia et Jure.* Lugduni, 1646.

Lyons, D. *Forms and Limits of Utilitarianism.* Oxford: Clarendon Press, 1965.

Mabbott, J. D. *An Introduction to Ethics.* London: Hutchinson University Library, 1966.

Maritain, J. *Man and the State.* Chicago: University of Chicago Press, 1951.

————. *Neuf Leçons sur les notions premières de la philosophie morale.* Paris: Pierre Tequi, 1949.

————. *On the Philosophy of History.* New York: Charles Scribner's Sons, 1957.

————. *La Philosophie morale.* Paris: Librarie Gallimard, 1960.

————. *The Rights of Man and Natural Law.* New York: Charles Scribner's Sons, 1943.

Martineau, J. *Types of Ethical Theory.* Oxford: Clarendon Press, 1898.

McKeon, R. P. "The Meanings of Justice and the Relations among Traditions of Thought," *Revue internationale de philosphie,* 41 (1957), 253–267.

————. "Justice and Equality," *Nomos VI,* pp. 44–61.

Melden, A. I. *Rights and Right Conduct.* Oxford: Basil Blackwell, 1959.

Messner, J. *Social Ethics: Natural Law in the Modern World.* St. Louis: B. Herder Book Co., 1965.

Mill, J. *Utilitarianism, Liberty, and Representative Government.* New York: E. P. Dutton & Co., 1951.

Molina, L. de. *Los seis libros de la justicia y el derecho.* Madrid: J. H. Cosano, 1941.

Montesquieu, C. *The Spirit of the Laws.* Translated by T. Nugent. New York: Hafner Publishing Co., 1949.

Morgenthau, H. J. "On Trying to be Just," *Commentary,* May, 1963, pp. 420–423.

Murray, J. C. *We Hold These Truths.* Garden City: Doubleday & Co., 1960.

Nelson, L. *System of Ethics.* New Haven: Yale University Press, 1956.

Nomos VI. Justice, ed. C. J. Friedrich, J. W. Chapman. New York: Atherton Press, 1963.

Nowell-Smith, P. H. *Ethics.* Baltimore: Penguin Books, 1961.

Olafson, F. (ed.). *Justice and Social Policy.* Englewood Cliffs, N.J.: Prentice-Hall, Inc., 1961.

Paine, T. *Basic Writings of Thomas Paine.* New York: Wiley Book Co., 1942.
Pareto, V. *The Mind and Society.* New York: Harcourt, Brace & World, Co., 1942.
Perelman, C. *The Idea of Justice and the Problem of Argument.* Translated by J. Petrie. London: Routledge & Kegan Paul, 1963.
———. "L'idée de justice dans ses rapports avec la morale, le droit, et la philosophie," in *Le droit naturel,* pp. 125–146.
———. "Justice," *Revue internationale de philosophie,* 41 (1957), 344–362.
———. "Justice and Justification," *Natural Law Forum,* 10 (1965), 1–20.
Petrone, I. *Filosofia del diritto.* Milan: A. Giuffre, 1950.
Piaget, J. *The Moral Judgment of the Child.* London: Routledge, Kegan Paul, 1932.
Pieper, J. *Justice.* Translated by L. E. Lynch. New York: Pantheon Books, 1965.
Piot, A. *Droit naturel et réalisme.* Paris: Librarie Generale de Droit, 1930.
Plato. *Gorgias,* ed. A. Croiset, L. Bodin. Paris: Les Belles Lettres, 1949.
———. *The Republic,* ed. E. Chambry. Paris: Les Belles Lettres, 1947.
———. *Laws,* ed. E. de Place. Paris: Les Belles Lettres, 1951.
Popper, K. S. *The Open Society and its Enemies.* New York: Harper Bros., 1945.
Potter, H. *The Quest for Justice.* London: Sweet & Maxwell, 1951.
Pound, R. *Jurisprudence.* St. Paul, Minn.: West Publishing Co., 1959.
Price, R. *Review of the Principal Questions in Morals,* ed. D. D. Raphael. Oxford University Press, 1948.
Prichard, H. A. *Moral Obligation.* Oxford: Clarendon Press, 1949.
Prior, A. N. *Logic and the Basis of Ethics.* Oxford: Clarendon Press, 1956.
Proudhon, P. J. *De la justice dans la révolution et dans l'église.* Paris, 1858.
Pufendorf, S. *Elementorum Jurisprudentiae Universalis Libri Duo.* Oxford: Clarendon Press, 1931.
———. *De jure naturae et gentium.* Francofurti: Off. Knochio-Eslingeriana, 1759.
Rachel, S. *De Jure Naturae et Gentium Dissertationes.* Washington, D.C.: The Carnegie Institution, 1916.
Radbruch, G. *Rechtsphilosophie.* Stuttgart: K. F. Koehler, 1950.
Radin, M. *Law as Logic and Experience.* New Haven: Yale University Press, 1940.
Raphael, D. D. "Equality and Equity," *Philosophy,* 21 (1946), 118–132.
———. "Justice and Liberty," *Proceedings of The Aristotelian Society,* 51 (1951).
———. *The Moral Sense.* Oxford: Oxford University Press, 1947.
Rawls, J. "Constitutional Liberty and the Concept of Justice," *Nomos VI.*
———. "Justice as Fairness," in Olafson (ed.), *Justice and Social Policy,* pp. 80–107.
———. "Legal Obligation and the Duty of Fair Play," in Hook (ed.), *Law and Philosophy,* pp. 3–18.
———. "The Sense of Justice," *The Philosophical Review,* 72 (1963), 281–305.
Réglade, M. *Valeur sociale et concepts juridiques.* Paris: Recueil Sirey, 1950.
Reinach, A. *Die apriorisehen Grundlagen des bürgerlichen Rechts.* Munich: Kesel Verlag, 1953.
Rescher, N. *Distributive Justice.* Indianapolis: Bobbs-Merrill, 1966.

Revue internationale de philosophie, 41 (1957): "La Justice."

Ritchie, D. G. *Natural Rights.* London: George Allen & Unwin Ltd., 1952.

Robilant, E. di. *Teoria e Ideologia nelle Dottrine delle Giustizia.* Turin: G. Giappichelli, 1964.

Rodriguez, A. J. *La Justicia. Investigaciones de Seminario.* Buenos Aires, 1932.

Rommen, H. A. *The Natural Law.* St. Louis: B. Herder Book Co., 1948.

Roshwald, M. "The Concept of Human Rights," *Philosophy and Phenomenological Research,* 19 (1959), 354–379.

Ross, A. *On Law and Justice.* Berkeley: University of California Press, 1959.

Ross, D. *The Right and Good.* Oxford: Oxford University Press, 1930.

Rumeln, M. *Die Gerechtigkeit.* Tubingen, 1920.

Runciman, W. G. and A. K. Sen. "Games, Justice, and the General Will," *Mind,* 74 (1965), 554–562.

Ryan, J. A. *A Living Wage.* New York: Macmillan Publishing Co., 1906.

St. Germain. *Dialogue between a Doctor of Divinity and a Student in the Laws of England.* London, 1622.

Sayre, P. (ed.). *Interpretations of Modern Legal Philosophies.* New York: Oxford University Press, 1947.

Schonfeld, W. *Uber die Gerechtigkeit.* Gottingen: Van denhoeck & Ruprecht, 1952.

Schopenhauer, A. *On the Basis of Morality.* Translated by E. F. Paine. Indianapolis: Liberal Arts Press, 1965.

Searle, J. R. "How to Derive 'Ought' from 'Is'," *Philosophical Review,* 73 (1964) 43–58.

Senn, F. *De la justice et du droit.* Paris: Recueil Sirey, 1927.

Shields, L. W. *The History and Meaning of the Term "Social Justice."* Notre Dame: Notre Dame University Press, 1941.

Siches, L. R. "Justicia," *Revue internationale de philosophie,* 41 (1957), 302–323.

Sidgwick, H. *Methods of Ethics.* 7th ed. London: Macmillan & Co., 1962.

Simon, Y. *The Philosophy of Democratic Government.* Chicago: University of Chicago Press, 1951.

―――. *The Tradition of Natural Law,* ed. V. Kuic. New York: Fordham University Press, 1965.

Singer, M. G. *Generalization in Ethics.* New York: Alfred A. Knopf, 1961.

Smith, A. *Lectures on Justice, Police, Revenues, and Arms.* New York: A. M. Kelley, 1965.

―――. *Theory of Moral Sentiments.* New York: A. M. Kelley, 1966.

Soto, D. *Libri X de Justitia et Jure.* Venice: B. Rubinam, 1573.

Sparshott, F. E. *An Enquiry into Goodness.* Toronto: Toronto University Press, 1958.

Spencer, H. *Social Statics.* New York: D. Appleton & Co., 1896.

Spinoza, B. de. "Tractatus Politicus," in *Writings on Political Philosophy,* ed. A. G. A. Balz. New York: Appleton, Century, Crofts, Inc., 1937.

Spir, A. "Recht und Unrecht," in *Gesammelte Schriften.* Stuttgart, 1884–85.

Stammler, R. *The Theory of Justice.* Translated by I. Husik. New York: Macmillan Co., 1925.

Stapleton, L. *Justice and World Society.* Chapel Hill, N.C.: University of North Carolina Press, 1944.

Stern, B. "Gerechtigkeit," *Archiv f. systematische Philosophie,* 10 (1904), 520 ff.

Stevenson, C. L. *Ethics and Language*. New Haven: Yale University Press, 1944.
——. "Persuasive Definitions," *Mind*, 47 (1938), 331–356.
Stone, J. *Human Law and Human Justice*. London: Stevens & Sons Ltd., 1965.
——. *The Province and Function of Law*. Sydney: Maitland Publications, 1961.
Strauss, L. *Natural Right and History*. Chicago: University of Chicago Press, 1953.
Stroll, A. *The Emotive Theory of Ethics*. Berkeley: University of California Press, 1954.
Suarez, F. *De legibus ac Deo legislatori*. Oxford: Clarendon Press, 1944.
Sweens, A. *De jure et justitia*. Haaren: C. N. Teulings, 1913.
Tammelo, I. "Justice and Doubt: An Essay on the Fundamentals of Justice," *Oesterreichische Zeitschrift für öffentliches Recht*, 9 (1958-59), 308–417.
Taparelli, L. *Saggio teoretico di dritto naturale appoggiato sul fatto*. Rome: Civiltà Cattolica, 1855.
Taylor, R. "Justice and The Common Good," in Hook (ed.), *Law and Philosophy*, pp. 86–97.
Tillich, P. *Love, Power, and Justice*. Oxford: Oxford University Press, 1954.
Tisset, P. "Les notions de Droit et de Justice," *Revue de metaphysique et Morale* (1930), pp. 66 ff.
Toulmin, S. *The Place of Reason in Ethics*. Cambridge: Cambridge University Press, 1964.
Tourtoulon, P. *Philosophy in the Development of Law*. New York: Macmillan Co., 1922.
——. *Les trois justices*. Paris: Recueil Sirey, 1933.
Utz, A. *Ethique sociale: Les principes de la doctrine sociale*. Fribourg: Editions Universitaires, 1958.
Vattel, E. *The Law of Nations on Principles of the Law of Nature*. London: G. G. & J. Robinson, 1797.
Vitoria, F. de. *De Justitia*. Madrid: Asociación F. de Vitoria, 1934.
Vlastos, G. "Justice," *Revue internationale de philosophie*, 41 (1957), 324–343.
——. "Justice and Equality," in Brandt, *Social Justice*, pp. 31–72.
Wellman, C. *The Language of Ethics*. Cambridge, Mass.: Harvard University Press, 1961.
Willoughby, W. W. *Social Justice*. New York, 1900.
Wilson, J. *Works*. Chicago: Callaghan & Co., 1896.
Wolff, C. *Jus Gentium methodo scientifica pertragtatum*. Oxford: Clarendon Press, 1934.
Von Wright, G. H. *The Varieties of Goodness*. London: Routledge & Kegan Paul, 1963.

Index

Amos, 45
Approbative character of justice, 10, 13–14, 30–32, 63, 101, 110, 144, 170
Aquinas, 3, 12, 18, 121, 122, 123, 125, 133, 134, 137, 139, 142, 145, 146, 152, 153, 154, 155, 158, 159, 166
Aristotle, 12, 18, 20, 121, 122, 123, 125, 129, 130, 134, 142, 152, 153, 157, 159
Augustine, 17, 120, 121
Austin, J. L., 18, 45, 46, 50, 56, 57, 58, 62, 63, 65, 73, 75, 81
Ayer, 45, 65

Basic theories or positions, 23, 28, 39, 163, 168–72
Baylis, 81
Benevolence, 112–16, 171
Bentham, J., 18, 81, 100, 109, 113
Blackstone, W., 121
Blanshard, B., 81, 99
Bobbio, N., 45
Bonum honestum, 33, 153
Brentano, F., 121, 144
Broad, C. D., 81, 93
Brown, Stuart M., 121, 133
Brunner, H. E., 121
Burke, Edmund, 121
Burlamaqui, J., 121
Bynkershoek, 120

Cicero, 121, 127, 158
Clark, 45
Common notes of justice, 10, 15–19, 21, 163, 167
Common subject of controversy, 9–10, 16, 17, 20, 163
Commutative justice, 5, 142

Complexity of basic theories, 164–68, 178
Conformity to law, justice as, 5–62, 82–85, 173–74
Conjugal justice, 143
Contract, 48, 70, 89, 96
Conventional character of justice, 27, 70 73, 80, 85–94, 129, 149, 178–80
Corrective justice, 5
Criminal justice, 5
Criterion of law, justice as, 26, 49, 54, 84, 131, 137–42, 173
Criterion of the state, justice as, 49–55

Debitum, 125, 126, 130, 150, 158
Declaration of Independence, 128, 139
Declaration of the Rights of Man and of the Citizen, 128
Definition of justice, 7, 9, 56, 67, 75, 95, 122, 123, 158, 164, 170
Del Vecchio, Giorgio, 5, 6, 12, 13, 21, 120
Despotic justice, 143
Desert, 16, 83, 97, 100, 135
Dialectical clarification, 6, 16, 18, 21, 34
Dialectical construction, 39, 45, 81, 121, 122
Dialectically difficult authors, 22, 41
Distribution, 8, 16, 27, 90, 93, 97, 114, 134
Distributive justice, 5, 53, 142
Divine law, 25, 50, 56, 59
Domestic justice, 5, 142
Due theory, 126
Duties, 17, 31, 54, 90, 114, 125, 127, 152, 179